Revisiting the FOUNDING ERA

READINGS FROM

THE GILDER LEHRMAN INSTITUTE OF AMERICAN HISTORY

EDITED BY CAROL BERKIN

THE GILDER LEHRMAN
INSTITUTE of AMERICAN HISTORY

New York, New York

This project has been made possible by a major grant from
the National Endowment for the Humanities.

THE GILDER LEHRMAN
INSTITUTE *of* AMERICAN HISTORY

49 West 45th Street, 2nd Floor, New York, NY 10036 · 646-366-9666

gilderlehrman.org

ISBN 978-1-932821-18-5

Contents

Section III: Creating the Constitution

Section IV: Governing the New Nation

Foreword

Why has the Gilder Lehrman Institute of American History decided to reissue the book *Revisiting the Founding Era* and distribute it free to thousands of schools? The answer might lie in the words of our revered trustee David McCullough, who has said that history is "an antidote to the hubris of the present." In particular, the courage and the perseverance of the founders, against all odds, have much to teach us. They had no idea how their dangerous endeavor would turn out, nor did they have, as Mr. McCullough writes, "any certainty of success":

> Had they taken a poll in Philadelphia in 1776, they would have scrapped the whole idea of independence. A third of the country was for it, a third of the country was against it, and the remaining third, in the old human way, was waiting to see who came out on top.
>
> (McCullough, *American Spirit*, Simon & Schuster, 2017)

On balance, most of us would agree that the outcome was a success, though never a perfect one. The tension between the ideals and the reality of America has been in discussion ever since.

Revisiting the Founding Era calls on Americans today to re-examine documents and ideas from that turbulent period with an eye to their endurance over time and their relevance in the twenty-first century. Supported by the National Endowment for the Humanities, and working in partnership with the American Library Association and the National Constitution Center, the Gilder Lehrman Institute enlisted four leading scholars of the era and the curators of the Gilder Lehrman Collection to compile this reader of twenty seminal documents, which is available in print and digital formats. They provided historical introductions and questions as the basis for classroom discussion, and the conversations that will arise elsewhere, across the country. By closely reading the documents and discussing them in class and beyond, students will gain insight into current issues through the lens of Founding Era controversies and compromises.

The Institute is making this reader available to thousands of teachers and students throughout the Gilder Lehrman Institute's network of Affiliate Schools, which in 2021 reached some 30,000 in number, touching the lives of five million students each year. Similarly, through the Hamilton Education Program, developed in partnership with Lin-Manuel Miranda and the Broadway musical *Hamilton*, and supported by The Rockefeller Foundation and other funders, the Gilder Lehrman Institute has since 2016 immersed more than 250,000 disadvantaged students in the Founding Era and helped them find their own connections to the people, issues, and events of the American past.

We hope to inspire not just the young but all readers to examine and appreciate the struggles, contributions, and legacies of the founders, and to engage with a renewed sense of purpose in the civic life of their community and their country today. Our deepest thanks go to distinguished scholar Professor Carol Berkin, Senior Advisor to the "Revisiting the Founding Era" project and General Editor of this volume. Special gratitude is also due to three other authorities on the Founding Era who contributed essays to this book: Professor Benjamin L. Carp, Professor Denver Brunsman, and Julie Silverbrook, JD.

The staff of the Gilder Lehrman Institute is deserving of recognition as well, chiefly Susan F. Saidenberg, former Senior Curator of Exhibitions and Public Programs, who served as Project Director. Offering their expertise in assembling and managing the reader were Nicole Seary, Senior Editor; Justine Ahlstrom, Executive Editor; and Sandra Trenholm, Director and Curator of the Gilder Lehrman Collection. Thanks are also due to Mindy DePalma, Director of Publications and Multimedia; Laura Hapke, Curatorial Outreach Coordinator; and Peter Shea, Senior Video Producer.

The entire "Revisiting the Founding Era" program of community conversations was supported by a generous grant from the Public Programs Division of the National Endowment for the Humanities, for which we are truly grateful. This reader, originally produced as part of the grant, will give students, educators, and other participants access to primary source documents that offer personal accounts and unique perspectives often left out of conventional history textbooks.

Our utmost appreciation and gratitude go to the late Richard Gilder and our Co-Chair Lewis E. Lehrman, founders of the Institute, whose vision and leadership have made possible all the programs at the Institute since its founding in 1994.

James G. Basker, President
The Gilder Lehrman Institute of American History

General Introduction

by

Carol Berkin

At first glance, the world of George Washington, Phillis Wheatley, and Alexander Hamilton shares little in common with twenty-first-century America. The founding fathers and mothers lived in a young and unproven nation, born in revolution and built upon principles of representative government and individual liberties that the older, more established nations of Europe viewed skeptically. No one, not even a visionary like Hamilton, could imagine that the United States would become a world leader, prosperous and powerful. What, then, can we learn from examining the founders' ideas and their actions? What can we discover if we read their words? How can the past help us understand our present? These are the questions this book seeks to address.

A close look suggests that there are many connections between the founders' world and our own. Throughout the eighteenth century, as colonists and later as citizens of an independent country, Americans were surrounded by rivals and enemies including France, Spain, and, after 1776, Great Britain. Today, threats to national security remain, similar to those faced by George Washington in his time. The issues raised in the halls of government, in the press, and in popular demonstrations, are also strikingly similar to those of the Founding Era.

Like Americans today, the founding generation confronted thorny issues, including the balance of power among the branches of government; the relative power of local and central government; the qualifications for full citizenship, suffrage, and office-holding; the tensions between law and order and the right to protest and demonstrate; the impact of taxation policies; the regulation of trade and commerce; race relations; and the interpretation of the Constitution.

Revisiting the Founding Era: Readings from the Gilder Lehrman Institute of American History is the centerpiece of a nationwide program for libraries supported by a generous grant from the National Endowment for the Humanities. Featuring a total of twenty core documents from the holdings of the Gilder Lehrman Institute, this reader offers you an opportunity to listen to the founding generation as it speaks to us across the centuries. It invites you to examine the challenges these men and women faced and the steps they took to meet them. And finally, it encourages you to engage in debate and discussion about the issues Americans confront today.

Revisiting the Founding Era is divided into four chronological sections: "Declaring Independence," "Realizing Independence," "Creating the Constitution," and "Governing the New Nation." Each section follows the same format: a brief introductory essay by a noted scholar followed by a selection of five documents—including letters, political writings, and poems—that provide insight into the momentous events and decisions of the eighteenth century through the eyes of those who participated in them. Each section is built around important themes that connect the introductory essay and the documents. Finally, each section includes questions that can serve as starting points for your conversations about documents and ideas that remain relevant today.

"Declaring Independence" has as its central theme the process of radical political and social change. How did a protest over the Stamp Tax grow into a demand for political independence? The introductory essay by Benjamin Carp describes the role of communication, persuasion, and even violence in mobilizing a popular revolutionary movement. It raises critical questions such as: How did the colonists go from subjects to revolutionaries, and through what modes of resistance? What methods of persuasion are the most effective in our modern society? What is the role of the United States as a beacon today?

"Realizing Independence" has as its central theme the complexities of the American Revolution. Both a war for independence and a civil war, the Revolution pitted loyalists against their patriot neighbors, and family members against one another. The clarion call for "liberty" and "freedom" spoke not only to White colonists but also, as Denver Brunsman points out, to enslaved people and to Native Americans. For all, it was a long home-front war that demanded sacrifices from soldiers and civilians. It had consequences for the relationships between men and women as well as slaveholders and enslaved people. This section raises a different set of critical questions: How do primary sources deepen our understanding of the birth of the country? What burdens do wars place on the civilian population? How has the treatment of veterans changed (or not) over time?

"Creating the Constitution" has as its central theme the steps by which an unprecedented form of government was framed by the delegates to the Constitutional Convention. As I explain in my introductory essay on this topic, many Americans opposed ratification of the document that these men produced. The section raises a number of questions for debate and discussion: What, if any, changes would your community like to see made to the Constitution—and how would you prefer these changes be made? What powers do you feel are best left to state or local governments, and what powers are best entrusted to the federal government? What are the popular forums for political discourse today?

"Governing the New Nation" has as its central theme the problems that arose in the first decade of the new federal government. Foreign threats, intense criticism of the government and of individual political leaders, economic difficulties, and the anxieties of citizens that their rights and liberties might be eroded all threatened the survival of the American experiment in self-government. Despite the intense disagreements between the Federalists and the Jeffersonian Republicans, Americans managed a peaceful transition of power in 1801 that set a precedent for a democracy that survives today. This section prompts a number of critical questions: How do the debates over free speech and national security that roiled the Founding Era persist today? Does the national government have the right to enforce its laws if states or groups of citizens reject them? How does your community view the process for electing a president and the role of the Electoral College?

Revisiting the Founding Era is designed to promote conversations about challenges in present-day American life. The questions posed in each section of the book are intended as starting points for discussion. These should be seen only as points of departure, for we know that each community has its own set of unique concerns and interests. We hope that the documents in this reader will serve not only as a window into the nation's past, but also as a framework for understanding the ideas that shaped the world in which we live today.

Chronology of the Founding Era

1765

Parliament imposes Stamp Act on American colonies

1768

British troops land in Boston

1769

Six Nations receive $10,000 for land in Pennsylvania (p. 7)

1770

Boston Massacre heightens anti-British sentiment

Paul Revere prints *The Bloody Massacre Perpetrated in King-Street, Boston*, depicting the killing of Crispus Attucks and other patriots (p. 8)

1773

Boston Tea Party defies monopoly of British East India Company

Phillis Wheatley becomes first African American woman to publish a book, *Poems on Various Subjects, Religious and Moral* (p. 9)

1774

First Continental Congress meets

1775

Battles of Lexington and Concord spark American Revolution

Second Continental Congress meets

George Washington selected as commander in chief of Continental Army

Mercy Otis Warren notes the escalating violence of the war (p. 21)

John Adams proposes three branches of government (p. 11)

1776

Thomas Paine publishes *Common Sense* (p. 13)

Declaration of Independence (p. 67)

1777

George Washington urges measures to raise troops and supplies (p. 23)

Lucy Flucker Knox writes to Henry Knox, detailing struggles on home front (p. 25)

British defeated at Saratoga, New York

Articles of Confederation drafted as nation's first form of government (p. 37)

1778

France signs treaty with United States, establishing military alliance

Timothy Pickering confirms commitment to American cause in letter to his loyalist father (p. 27)

1779

Spain declares war on England, supporting American Revolution

1781

Articles of Confederation ratified

American victory at Yorktown, Virginia

1783

Newburgh Conspiracy, a plot among aggrieved Continental Army officers, quelled by George Washington

George Washington issues circular letter to the states on securing the nation's future (p. 39)

Treaty of Paris signed, ending American Revolution

1786

Shays' Rebellion, an armed revolt of Massachusetts farmers, exposes weaknesses of Articles of Confederation

1787

George Washington observes need for strong central government (p. 41)

Constitutional Convention

Northwest Ordinance outlaws slavery in western territories

US Constitution drafted (p. 52)

Mercy Otis Warren assesses the question of ratification in letter to Catharine Macaulay (p. 43)

James Madison, John Jay, and Alexander Hamilton write and serially publish the Federalist Papers

Henry Knox expresses support for US Constitution in letter to Marquis de Lafayette (p. 45)

1788

Ratification of US Constitution

1789

Electoral College selects George Washington as first President of the United States

1790

Alexander Hamilton presents his financial plan in *Report . . . [on] the Public Credit* (p. 55)

1791

Ratification of Bill of Rights

1794

Whiskey Rebellion among anti-tax protesters in Pennsylvania suppressed by federal militia

1796

George Washington issues Farewell Address, warning against political factions and foreign entanglements

1797

John Adams inaugurated as second President

1798

Quasi-War with France begins

Alien and Sedition Acts passed, permitting deportation of non-Americans and stifling opposition to federal government

1799

George Washington rejects pleas to run for presidency in 1800 (p. 57)

Washington dies

1800

Publication of *Communications from Several States, on the Resolutions of the Legislature of Virginia,* denouncing Alien and Sedition Acts (p. 61)

Gabriel's Rebellion, a planned uprising of enslaved people in Richmond, Virginia, is foiled, leading to execution of Gabriel Prosser and his followers

Alexander Hamilton supports Thomas Jefferson over Aaron Burr in contested presidential election (p. 59)

1801

Thomas Jefferson sworn in as third President

1803

Louisiana Purchase doubles size of United States

1806

Formerly enslaved Revolutionary War veteran Peter Kiteredge petitions Massachusetts legislators for aid (p. 29)

1808

Britain and America ban the transatlantic slave trade

Section I

DECLARING INDEPENDENCE

Engraved portrait of Phillis Wheatley,
frontispiece of *Poems on Various Subjects, Religious and Moral,* London, 1773
(The Gilder Lehrman Institute of American History, GLC06154)

Section I

Declaring Independence

by Benjamin L. Carp

DOCUMENTS

- Receipt for land purchased from the Six Nations, July 28, 1769
- *The Bloody Massacre Perpetrated in King-Street, Boston*, an engraving by Paul Revere, 1770
- "On Being Brought from Africa to America" from *Poems on Various Subjects, Religious and Moral* by Phillis Wheatley, 1773
- *from* John Adams to Richard Henry Lee outlining the executive, legislative, and judicial branches of American government, November 15, 1775
- from *Common Sense* by Thomas Paine, 1776

A. OVERVIEW

Governing the British Empire was tough. After its victory over France in 1763, Great Britain had twenty-six colonies in the Western Hemisphere alone. Britain faced heavy war debts and continuing military commitments. It had to maintain a vast trading empire and govern a variety of Black, Native American, Asian, and White subjects. Meanwhile, the American colonies had their own legislative assemblies that made laws and levied taxes, so they were reluctant to accept additional taxes passed by the British Parliament. By 1775, crises over land, trade, and taxation led to a widespread war of rebellion in thirteen of these colonies.

In 1763, the king forbade his colonists from settling west of the Appalachian Mountains, a measure intended to pacify Indian-White relations. The British Army was needed to maintain newly conquered territories and protect revenue officers in the cities. The soldiers' presence caused several conflicts with Americans who wanted to move westward and resented having to pay for military upkeep. Outspoken colonists complained about new taxes levied by the British Parliament (where they weren't represented), such as a stamp tax required for a variety of legal documents, newspapers, and other items (1765) and taxes on paper, lead, glass, painter's colors, and tea (1767). These colonists began to question how much authority Parliament ought to have over the American colonies. It was an attitude the authorities refused to accept.

When Bostonians dumped forty-six tons of the East India Company's tea into the harbor in 1773, Parliament responded with the Coercive Acts of 1774, which shut the port of Boston until it paid for the lost tea, reduced the power of Massachusetts town meetings, made the city's council appointed rather than chosen by the legislature, and moved trials of government officials to England. In response, the thirteen colonies between Georgia and New England began drilling the militia, establishing committees of correspondence to halt trade with the mother country, and sending delegates to the First Continental Congress. When Massachusetts governor Thomas Gage moved to seize arms and ammunition from the countryside on April 19, 1775, fights broke out at Lexington and Concord. Bloodshed made reconciliation increasingly difficult.

Even after this, many American colonists were reluctant to embrace the movement for independence—indeed, some never did, and remained loyalists throughout the war. The delegates to the Continental Congress who favored a radical break had to convince their fellow colonists to declare independence from Great Britain.

B. THEMES

1. Communication and Persuasion

The British Empire ordered soldiers to Boston in 1768 to protect revenue-collecting officials from local crowds. Uneasy relations between civilians and soldiers ultimately led to the so-called "Boston Massacre" of 1770. The image of British soldiers firing on Bostonians was a powerful piece of propaganda, and colors the way Americans remember the Revolution, much as images of violent protest (and counterprotest) become indelible today. Paul Revere's engraving of the Boston Massacre (1770) shows how patriot leaders used words and images to build a movement for resistance (and, later, independence). Revere's print shows how important it was for the patriot movement to create enduring narratives in order to galvanize followers, persuade the indecisive, and intimidate the enemy. The actual history of the Boston Massacre is more complex than Revere's one-sided engraving would suggest: many Bostonians got along amiably with the British soldiers in their midst, and on the night of March 5, 1770, the Boston crowd did a great deal to provoke the soldiers' violence by hurling projectiles at the troops.

2. Mobilizing for Independence

Through networks of letter writers, newspapers, town meetings, spinning bees, boycotts, and other methods, the revolutionaries enabled men and women to imagine themselves as defending American rights—and eventually to imagine the United States as an independent nation in its own right. Thomas Paine's *Common Sense* (1776) convinced many Americans to accept the radical argument for independence from Great Britain. Paine understood the importance of using the printed word to unite far-flung Americans in a common cause.

Paine warned against continued connections with Great Britain because such ties would drag America into European wars. Instead, America had a "duty to mankind at large" to pursue friendship and trade with other nations, and to be "the asylum for the persecuted lovers of civil and religious liberty from *every part* of Europe." Paine believed that an oppressive government was worse than no government at all.

Paine also wanted Americans to liberate themselves from monarchy and aristocracy. He believed that a republican government would better ensure justice and equality, even in an imperfect world.

3. Nation Making and State Making

John Adams's letter to Richard Henry Lee on November 15, 1775, makes clear that the leading founders wanted to build a government that would support America's different economic interests, provide security and defense, and prove worthy of international recognition.

Initially, committees of safety and provincial conventions acted as new governing bodies. While today we admire the seemingly democratic quality of these local institutions, these committees often used their power in abusive ways. Today we think of state authority being embodied by an enormous federal government supported by a technologically advanced military apparatus, but we might also look at how local governments balance authority and liberty.

In Adams's day, these committees and conventions conceded a lot of power to leading magistrates. While the lower house would be popularly elected, all of the other branches of government (the council, the governor, and judges) were appointed by a smaller elite body, and there were several "veto points" that might thwart the popular will. Judges did not have to face the electorate, and armed forces were controlled by the governor. The colonists were not yet accustomed to independence or republican government, so Adams suggested relatively familiar forms of government. Months before Jefferson drafted the Declaration of Independence, other delegates to Congress had already laid out a blueprint for new governments.

4. Race

Not all Americans benefited from independence. The ideal of freedom and equality promised by the Revolution did not extend to American Indians or African Americans. A 1769 document records that colonists paid representatives of the Six Nations $10,000 for land. This is the most that had ever been paid for American Indian land, and today, it looks like a lopsided exchange. The negotiation set the stage for future conflicts that would come to fruition during Dunmore's War (1774) and the Revolutionary War. The American revolutionaries' desire for independence was born in part of a desire to settle on American Indian lands without further interference from the British Empire. And yet at the same time, the document shows how powerful eastern American Indian groups like the Iroquois, or Haudenosaunee, were able to play the game of negotiating, fighting, and working with colonists all the way to the end of the eighteenth century and beyond.

With talk of liberty in the air, few felt the lack of freedom more acutely than the men and women who were enslaved, vulnerable to corporal punishment, sexual assault, and the sundering of their families. In 1773, Phillis Wheatley, who had been captured in Africa as a child and sold into slavery in Boston, published *Poems on Various Subjects, Religious and Moral* (1773). In poems such as "On Being Brought from Africa to America," she challenges racism, reminding Christians that "Negros, black as Cain, / May be refin' d, and join th' angelic train."

C. QUESTIONS

1. One of the most remarkable things about the period 1763–1775 is how the colonists went from being willing participants in a triumphant British empire to arming themselves against the minions of the British Crown. How did this come about? How did activism and coalition building sustain the resistance movement and bring about the push for independence?
2. How do shocking images travel through social networks to galvanize political movements?
3. What is America's "duty to mankind at large," viewed by Thomas Paine as the bedrock of the nation? Has the US always comported itself as an asylum for the persecuted?

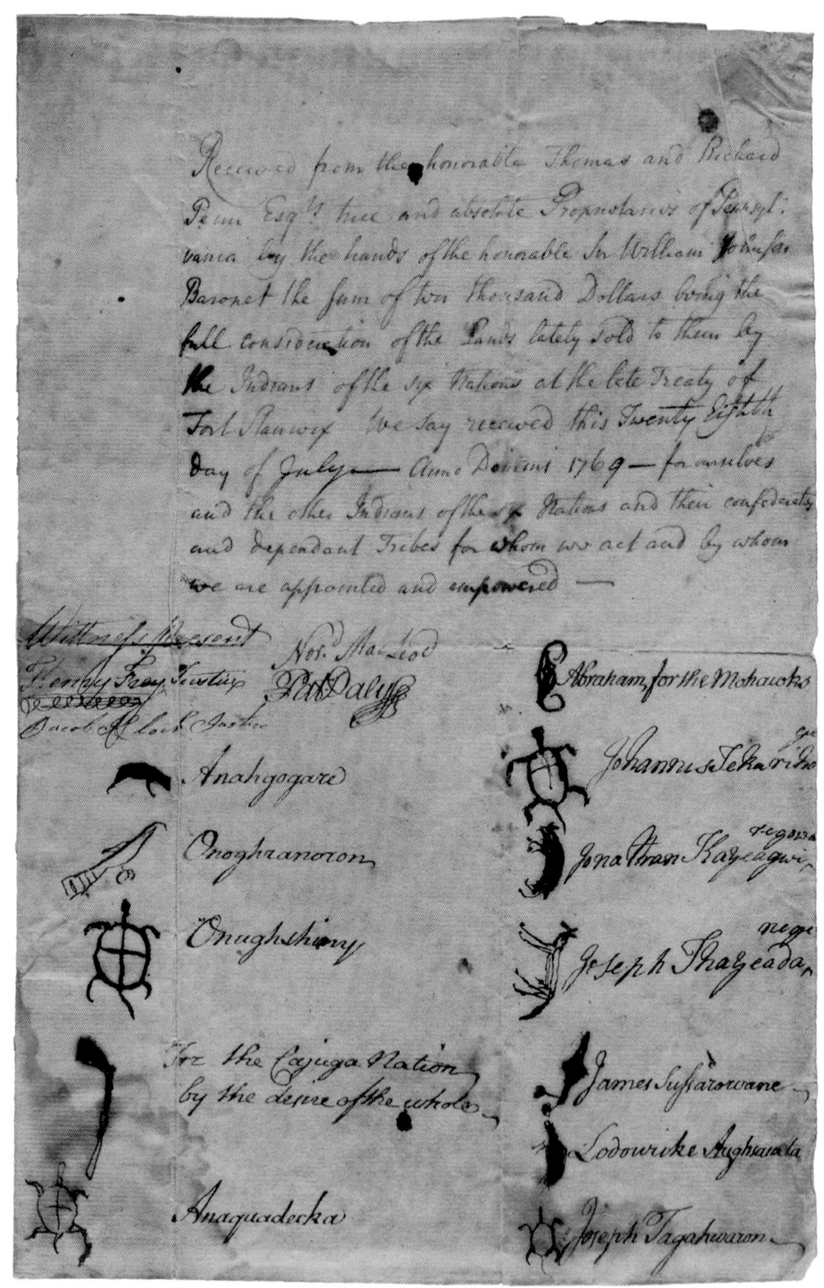

Received from the honorable Thomas and Richard Penn Esq.rs true and absolute Proprietaries of Pennsylvania by the hands of the honorable Sir William Johnson Baronet the sum of ten thousand Dollars being the full consideration of the Lands lately sold to them by the Indians of the Six Nations at the late Treaty of Fort Stanwix We say received this Twenty Eighth Day of July — Anno Domini 1769 — for ourselves and the other Indians of the Six Nations and their confederates and dependant Tribes for whom we act and by whom we are appointed and empowered —

Witness present
Nor. MacLeod
Pat Daly
Henry Frey Justice
Jacob Klock Justice

Anahgogare
Onoghranoron
Onughshiony
For the Cajuga Nation by the desire of the whole
Anaquaderka

Abraham, for the Mohawks
Johannes Tekarihoga
Jonathan Kayeagwiregowa
Joseph Thayeadanegea
James Sussarowane
Lodowicke Aughsarada
Joseph Tagahwaron

Document signed with the totems of fourteen chiefs of the Six Nations of the Iroquois (Haudenosaunee), July 28, 1769
(The Gilder Lehrman Institute of American History, GLC02548, p. 1)

THE SIX NATIONS OF THE IROQUOIS (HAUDENOSAUNEE)

Receipt for land purchased from the Six Nations by Pennsylvania, signed by fourteen chiefs, July 28, 1769

This document records that the representatives of the Six Nations, who signed using totems to designate individuals and tribes, received $10,000 as payment for land the tribes had ceded in the Treaty of Fort Stanwix in 1768. The British authorities hoped to prevent further conflicts between White settlers and American Indians by forbidding the continued migration of White settlers and paying for lands they had already occupied. After giving up their land, the Six Nations dispersed, with some staying in western New York and others traveling north to Canada and west to Wisconsin. This dispossession of the Native American peoples is an integral part of the story of European colonization of the Americas, beginning with the first Spanish incursions in the late fifteenth century.

Received from the honorable Thomas and Richard Penn Esq^{rs}. true and absolute Proprietaries of Pennsylvania by the hands of the honorable Sir William Johnson Baronet the sum of ten thousand Dollars being the full consideration of the Lands lately sold to them by the Indians of the six Nations at the late Treaty of Fort Stanwix We say received this Twenty Eighth day of July—Anno Domini 1769—for ourselves and the other Indians of the six Nations and their confederates and dependant Tribes for whom we act and by whom we are appointed and empowered—

Wittness Present	Nord. MacLeod		
Henry Frey Justice	Pat: Daly	[totem image]	Abraham, for the Mohawks
Jacob K. Cook Justice			
[totem image]	Anahgogare	[totem image]	Johannes Tekaridoge
[totem image]	Onoghranoron	[totem image]	Jonathan Kayeagwiregowa
[totem image]	Onughshiny	[totem image]	Joseph Thayeadanege
[totem image]	For the Cajuga Nation by the desire of the whole–	[totem image]	James Sussarowane—
[totem image]	Anaquadecka	[totem image]	Lodowicke Aughsawata
		[totem image]	Joseph Tagahwaron—
[totem image]	Serrehoana		
[totem image]	Sayuni		

PAUL REVERE (1735–1818)

The Bloody Massacre Perpetrated in King-Street, Boston on March 5th, 1770, by a Party of the 29th Reg., 1770

This hand-colored engraving by Paul Revere, artisan and patriot, elevates a street skirmish in Boston in 1770 into a "Massacre." A brilliant piece of propaganda, it galvanized the colonists' sentiments against repressive policies of the British.

Paul Revere, *The Bloody Massacre Perpetrated in King-Street, Boston*, 1770
(The Gilder Lehrman Institute of American History, GLC01868)

PHILLIS WHEATLEY (ca. 1753–1784)

"On Being Brought from Africa to America" (1773)

Born in Africa, Phillis Wheatley was captured as a child and sold into slavery in Boston. After impressing her owners with her genius, she was privately educated in several subjects and began publishing poetry as a teenager.

In her most famous poem, Wheatley expresses her view that it was God's larger plan for her salvation, rather than the wickedness of slave traders, that determined the events of her life. Still, she undermines White complacency, reminding Christians (with an apt pun on sugarcane processing) that Blacks and Whites are equal in the divine plan.

On being brought from AFRICA to AMERICA.

'TWAS mercy brought me from my *Pagan* land,
Taught my benighted ſoul to underſtand
That there's a God, that there's a *Saviour* too:
Once I redemption neither ſought nor knew.
Some view our ſable race with ſcornful eye,
"Their colour is a diabolic die."
Remember, *Chriſtians*, *Negros*, black as *Cain*,
May be refin'd, and join th' angelic train.

On

Phillis Wheatley, *Poems on Various Subjects, Religious and Moral*, 1773
(The Gilder Lehrman Institute of American History, GLC06154, p. 18)

John Adams

Philadelphia Novr 15th 1775

Dear Sir The Course of Events, naturally turns the Thoughts of Gentlemen to the Subjects of Legislation and Jurisprudence, and it is a curious Problem what Form of Government, is most readily & easily adopted by a Colony, upon a Sudden Emergency. Nature and Experience have already pointed out the Solution of this Problem, in the Choice of Conventions and Committees of Safety. Nothing is wanting in Addition to these to make a compleat Government, but the Appointment of Magistrates for the due Administration of Justice.

Taking Nature and Experience for my Guide I have made the following Sketch, which may be varied in any one particular an infinite Number of Ways, So as to accommodate it to the different Genius, Temper, Principles and even Prejudices of different People.

A Legislative, an Executive and a judicial Power, comprehend the whole of what is meant and understood by Government. It is by ballancing each of these Powers against the other two, that the Effort in humane Nature towards Tyranny, can alone be checked and restrained and any degree of Freedom preserved in the Constitution.

Let a full and free Representation of the People be chosen for an House of Commons.

Let the House choose by Ballott twelve, Sixteen, Twenty four or Twenty Eight Persons, either Members of the House, or from the People at Large as the Electors please, for a Council.

John Adams to Richard Henry Lee, November 15, 1775
(The Gilder Lehrman Institute of American History, GLC03864, p. 1)

JOHN ADAMS (1735–1826)

from Letter to Richard Henry Lee, November 15, 1775

On the evening of November 14, 1775, Richard Henry Lee, a delegate to the Continental Congress from Virginia, visited John Adams at his Philadelphia residence. The two men discussed which form of government might be easily adopted by the colonies. Lee requested that Adams write down his plan and then circulate copies of the letter to convince colonists that independence would not be as difficult as they feared.

In this excerpt from a letter written the following day, Adams outlines the government that he envisions for America, with executive, legislative, and judicial branches, similar to the colonial government of Massachusetts. He also argues for a bicameral legislature and insists that judges not have overlapping offices in the other branches.

Philadelphia Nov[r] 15th.1775

Dear Sir

The Course of Events, naturally turns the Thoughts of Gentlemen to the Subjects of Legislation and Jurisprudence, and it is a curious Problem what Form of Government, is most readily & easily adopted by a Colony, upon a Sudden Emergency. Nature and Experience have already pointed out the Solution of this Problem, in the Choice of Conventions and Committees of Safety. Nothing is wanting in Addition to these to make a compleat Government, but the Appointment of Magistrates for the due Administration of Justice.

taking Nature and Experience for my Guide I have made the following Sketch, which may be varied in any one particular an infinite Number of Ways, So as to accommodate it to the different, Genius, Temper, Principles and even Prejudices of different People.

A Legislative, an Executive and a judicial Power, comprehend the whole of what is meant and understood by Government. It is by ballancing each of these Powers against the other two, that the Effort in human Nature towards Tyranny can alone be checked and restrained and any degree of Freedom preserved in the Constitution.

Let a full and free Representation of the People be chosen for an House of Commons.

Let the House choose by Ballott twelve, Sixteen, Twenty four or Twenty Eight Persons, either Members of the House or from the People at large as the Electors please, for a Council.

Let the House and Council by joint Ballott choose a Governor, annually triennially or Septennially as you will.

Let the Governor, Council, and House be each a distinct and independent Branch of the Legislature, and have a Negative on all Laws. . . .

Let the Judges, at least of the Supreme Court, be incapacitated by Law from holding any Share of the Legislative or Executive Power, Let their Commissions be during good Behaviour, and their Salaries ascertained and established by Law.

COMMON SENSE;

ADDRESSED TO THE

INHABITANTS

OF

AMERICA,

On the following interefting

SUBJECTS:

I. Of the Origin and Defign of Government in general, with concife Remarks on the Englifh Conftitution.
II. Of Monarchy and Hereditary fucceffion.
III. Thoughts on the Prefent State of American Affairs.
IV. Of the prefent Ability of America, with fome mifcellaneous Reflections.

A NEW EDITION, with feveral Additions in the Body of the Work. To which is added, an APPENDIX; together with an Addrefs to the People called QUAKERS.

N. B. The New Edition here given increafes the Work upwards of One-Third.

By THOMAS PAINE,

Secretary to the Committee for Foreign Affairs to Congrefs, during the American War, and Author of The Rights of Man, and a Letter to the Abbe Raynal.

LONDON:

PRINTED FOR H. D. SYMONDS, PATERNOSTER-ROW.

1793.

(PRICE SIX-PENCE.)

Thomas Paine, *Common Sense* (1776, reprinted 1793)
(The Gilder Lehrman Institute of American History, GLC08643)

THOMAS PAINE (1737–1809)

from *Common Sense* (Philadelphia, 1776; repr. London, 1793), pp. 13-14.

Described by historian Gordon S. Wood as "the most incendiary and popular pamphlet of the entire revolutionary era," Thomas Paine's *Common Sense* was the first work to call for independence from Great Britain. Writing in plain language for a wide readership, Paine published *Common Sense* anonymously because of its subversive content. In this passage, he argues that the American colonists have nothing to gain by remaining politically and economically connected to the mother country.

But Britain is the parent country, say some. Then the more shame upon her conduct. Even brutes do not devour their young, nor savages make war upon their families: wherefore the assertion, if true, turns to her reproach; but it happens not to be true, or only partly so, and the phrase *parent* or *mother country* hath been jesuitically adopted by the [King] and his parasites, with a low papistical design of gaining an unfair bias on the credulous weakness of our minds. Europe and not England is the parent country of America. This new world hath been the asylum for the persecuted lovers of civil and religious liberty from *every part* of Europe. Hither have they fled, not from the tender embraces of the mother, but from the cruelty of the monster; and it is so far true of England, that the same tyranny which drove the first emigrants from home, pursues their descendants still. . . .

I challenge the warmest advocate for reconciliation, to shew a single advantage that this continent can reap by being connected with Great Britain; I repeat the challenge, not a single advantage is derived. Our corn will fetch its price in any market in Europe, and our imported goods must be paid for, buy them where we will.

But the injuries and disadvantages we sustain by that connection, are without number; and our duty to mankind at large, as well as to ourselves, instruct us to renounce the alliance. Because, any submission to, or dependance on Great Britain, tends directly to involve this continent in European wars and quarrels, and set us at variance with nations, who would otherwise seek our friendship, and against whom we have neither anger nor complaint. As Europe is our market for trade, we ought to form no partial connection with any part of it. It is the true interest of America to steer clear of European contentions, which she never can do, while by her dependence on Britain, she is made the make-weight in the scale of British politics.

Section II

REALIZING INDEPENDENCE

George Washington by Rembrandt Peale, ca. 1853
(The Gilder Lehrman Institute of American History, GLC09119.01)

Section II

Realizing Independence

by Denver Brunsman

DOCUMENTS

- *from* Mercy Otis Warren to Catharine Macaulay regarding the barbarity of the British, August 24, 1775
- *from* George Washington to the President of the Convention of New Hampshire requesting troops and supplies, January 23, 1777
- *from* Lucy Flucker Knox to Henry Knox on daily life and family, August 23, 1777
- Timothy Pickering to Timothy Pickering Sr. expressing happiness over an improvement in his father's health and regret over their political differences, February 23, 1778
- Peter Kiteredge, Petition to the Selectmen of Medfield, Massachusetts, April 26, 1806

A. OVERVIEW

The American Revolutionary War was one of the hardest fought conflicts in the nation's history. Per capita the war involved the third highest mobilization rate of military-age men (trailing only World War II and the Civil War) and second highest casualty rate (after the Civil War) of all wars in American history. Moreover, the Revolutionary War was long, stretching for eight and a half years from 1775 to 1783. Only three other wars in American history were longer: the country's recent wars in Vietnam, Iraq, and Afghanistan.

The Revolutionary War had two distinct halves. The first half of the war, fought from the spring of 1775 to the winter of 1777–1778, took place primarily in North America and centered on the American colonial rebellion against the British Empire. General George Washington, commander of the American forces, overcame a major defeat at New York in August 1776 to lead inspiring victories against the British at Trenton (December 1776) and Princeton (January 1777). Unable to extinguish the rebellion, the British were left to capture leading American seaports, including New York and Philadelphia, before suffering a defeat at Saratoga, New York, in October 1777.

America's victory at Saratoga convinced Britain's foremost rival, France, to enter the war on the American side. The Franco-American alliance, made official in February 1778, marked the opening of the second half of the war. No longer simply a colonial conflict, the American Revolution expanded into a global war that would also include Spain and the Netherlands fighting against Britain. With so many enemies, Britain and its famed Royal Navy lost control of the seas for the first time during the eighteenth century; not coincidentally, Britain also lost its only war in the century. In October 1781, French army and naval forces aided Washington's Continental Army in forcing British general Charles Cornwallis to surrender at Yorktown, Virginia. Two years later, American and British diplomats signed the Treaty of Paris, which recognized the independence of the United States of America.

Today, it is easy to take American independence for granted, but it was hardly ensured. Indeed, if the primary documents on the war from the Gilder Lehrman Collection share one overriding theme, it is sacrifice. The war caused not only bloodshed but other forms of loss and division in American society. As difficult as it was to declare independence, American colonists discovered that realizing independence was even harder.

B. THEMES

1. Onset of the War

Of all the misconceptions about the American Revolution, perhaps the most common is that independence preceded war. In fact, the war came first and helped lead to independence.

In a letter to the British historian Catharine Macaulay, the American writer and patriot Mercy Otis Warren describes in vivid detail the scene around Boston in the summer following the start of the war at Lexington and Concord in April 1775. Warren extols "the Bravery of the Peasants of Lexington, & the spirit of freedom Breath'd from the Inhabitants of the surrounding Villages." Warren's passion against the "Wanton Barbarity" of the British illustrates how the war pushed Americans to support independence by 1776.

2. The Home Front

The War of Independence was not just a revolutionary war but also a civil war. Rather than entire regions fighting against each other, as in the American Civil War, individuals often fought neighbors and even family members during the Revolution.

Timothy Pickering, a future secretary of state in the Washington and Adams administrations, fought on the American side in the Revolution. His father, Timothy Pickering Sr., stayed loyal to the British Crown. In February 1778, Pickering learned that his father was gravely ill and wrote an affectionate letter seeking reconciliation. Pickering appreciated his father for allowing the "freedom in thinking & the rights of conscience" that made their differences possible. Pickering Sr. died a few months later.

The human side of the war also comes through in a letter from Lucy Knox to her husband, Henry Knox, a general in the Continental Army, in August 1777. Lucy recounts her loneliness and "solitary" life in Boston, as her immediate family remained loyal to Britain and fled the town while Henry was away fighting on the American side. There was a silver lining, however, as women like Lucy Knox managed their households and experienced new opportunities with their husbands gone—a phenomenon repeated in later American wars, and famously represented in the figure of Rosie the Riveter in World War II. Lucy did not want everything to return to normal after the war. "I hope you will not consider yourself as commander in chief of your own house," she writes to Henry, "but be convinced . . . that there is such a thing as equal command."

3. Unequal Hardships

The American Revolution inaugurated another feature of future American wars. Common people, particularly the poor, experienced the greatest hardships. As early as January 1777, George Washington understood this fact, as evidenced by his letter calling on the state of New Hampshire to fulfill its troop allotment set by Congress. Washington wrote, "You must be fully sensible of the Hardship imposed upon Individuals, and how detrimental it must be to the Public, to have her Farmers and Tradesmen frequently called into the Field as Militia-men." Yet he justified the sacrifice as necessary, lest America "submit to a greater [inconvenience], the total

Loss of our Liberties." Although future generations of Americans would appreciate this rationale, the Continental Army faced recruiting shortages throughout the Revolution.

4. Treatment of Veterans

Since the Revolution, every generation of Americans has confronted the question of how best to treat the nation's veterans. The question carries particular meaning for the Founding Era in light of the extraordinary sacrifices made by soldiers in the Revolutionary War.

The final document in this section is an appeal by the African American veteran Peter Kiteredge to the local government of Medfield, Massachusetts, for aid to support his wife and four children. Formerly enslaved, Kiteredge served as a private for five years in the American military (presumably the Continental Army) before later working as a sailor and laborer. During the Revolution, he sustained injuries, for which he "suffered in a greater or less degree ever since." We do not know the outcome of his request for help.

C. QUESTIONS

1. How do Revolutionary War casualty statistics and firsthand accounts of hardship by Lucy Knox, George Washington, Peter Kiteredge, and others change your understanding of the country's founding?
2. How was the experience of American men and women during the Revolution similar to or different from the experience of war today?
3. In what ways has the treatment of veterans changed (or not changed) since the Revolutionary War?

Plimouth N E August 24 1775

At a time when all Europe is Interested in the state of America you will forgive me Dear Madam if I lay aside the Ceremony usually observed where there is no Attachment that Arises Either from Affection or Esteem, & again Call of your Attention when I have Not been Assured of the Welcome Reception of my Last. in that I hinted that the sword was half Drawn from the scabbard. soon after which this people were obliged to unsheath it to Repel the Violence offered to Individuals, & the Insolence of an Attempt to seize the private property of the subjects of the king of England. And thereby put it out of their power to Defend themselves against the Corrupt Ministers of His Court. You have Doubtless, Madam been Apprized of the Consequences of this Hostile Movement which compelled the Americans to fly to arms in Defence of all that is held dear & sacred among Mankind. And the public papers as well as private accounts have Witnessed to the Bravery of the peasants of Lexington & the spirit of freedom Breathed from the Inhabitants of the surrounding Villages. You have been told of the Distresses of the people of Boston. And the shameful Violation of faith which will Leave a stain on the Memory of A Certain General officer as Long as the obligations of Honour & Truth are held sacred among Men. He after sporting with the Miseries of the Wretched sufferers

Mercy Otis Warren to Catharine Macaulay, August 24, 1775
(The Gilder Lehrman Institute of American History, GLC01800.02, p. 1)

MERCY OTIS WARREN (1728–1814)

from Letter to Catharine Macaulay, August 24, 1775

Born and raised in Massachusetts, Mercy Otis Warren supported the patriot cause during the Revolutionary War and corresponded with its leaders, including John Adams. Her published writings include a volume of political poems (1790) and her masterwork, *History of the Rise, Progress and Termination of the American Revolution* (1805).

Warren wrote this letter to the English historian Catharine Macaulay to give her a true picture of the suffering of the colonists at the hands of the British. She praises "the Bravery of the peasants of Lexington" and describes the beginnings of representative government in Massachusetts.

Plimouth N E August 24 1775

At A time when all Europe is Interested in the fate of America you will forgive me Dear Madam, if I . . . again Call of your Attention when I have Not been Assured of the Welcome Reception of my Last. in that I hinted that the sword was half Drawn from the scabbard, soon after which this people were obliged to unsheath it to Repel the Violence offered to Individuals. & the Insolence of an Attempt to seize the private property of the subjects of the king of England. And thereby put it out of their power to Defend themselves against the Corrupt Ministers of His Court.

You have Doubtless Madam been Apprized of the Consequences of this Hostile Movement which compeled the Americans to fly to arms in Defence of all that is held dear & sacred among Mankind. And the public papers as well as private accounts have Witnessed to the Bravery of the Peasants of Lexington. & the spirit of freedom Breath'd from the Inhabitants of the surrounding Villages. You have been told of the Distresses of the people of Boston . . . Famine & pestilence began to Rage in the City . . .

And the Conflagration of Charlestown will undoubtedly Reach Each British Ear before this comes to your Hand. Such Instances of Wanton Barbarity have been seldom practiced Even among the Most Rude & uncivilized Nations. the ties of Gratitude which were Broken through by the kings troops in this Base translation Greatly Enhances their Guilt. . . . We have a well Appointed Brave & High spirited Continental army, Consisting of About twenty two thousand Men, Commanded by the Accomplished George Washington Eq[r.] A Gentleman of one of the first Fortunes in America. A man whose Military Abilities, & public & private Virtues place Him in the first Class of the Good & Brave & are Really of so High a stamp as to do Honour to Human Nature. this army is to be occasionally Reunited & to be supported & paid at the Expence of The United Colonies of America. And were Britain powerful & Infatuated Enough to send out a force sufficiant to cut of to A Man this little Resolute army. Less than the Compass of A week would Exhibit in the Field thrice their Numbers Ready to Avenge the stroke & to call down the justice of Heaven on the Destroyers of the peace, Liberty & Happiness of Mankind.

In Compliance with the Recommendation of the Continental Congress the Massachusets have at Last Reassumed the powers of Government. the provincial Congress sent out A writ for Calling a House of Representatives & Agreable to the Charter of Wm & Mary they proceeded to Elect 28 Counselers. . . . Thus after Living without Goverment without Law and Without any Regular Administration of justice for more than 12 Months we are just Returning from a state of Nature to the subordinations of Civil Society.

Head Quart.rs Morris Town Jany 23d 1777

The Situation to which I am reduced for want of a Regular body of Troops on whom I can depend for a length of time, makes it indispensably necessary for me to call upon You and intreat you to exert Yourselves in levying and equipping the number of Battalions allotted to your State by the Resolution of Congress in September last.

You must be fully sensible of the Hardship imposed upon Individuals, and how detrimental it must be to the Public, to have her Farmers and Tradesmen frequently called into the Field as Militia-men, whereby a total Stop is put to Arts & Agriculture, without which We can not possibly long subsist. But great as this Inconvenience is, We must put up with it, or submit to a greater, the total Loss of our Liberties, untill our regular Continental Army can be brought into the Field.

The above Reasons alone I hope will be sufficient to induce you to exert Yourselves; for if our new Army are not ready to take the Field early in the Spring, We shall lose all the Advantages which I may say We have providentially gained this Winter. While our dependance is upon Militia, We have a full Army one day & scarce any the next; and I am much afraid, that the Enemy one day or other, taking Advantage of one of these temporary Weaknesses, will make themselves Masters of our Magazines of Stores, Arms & Artillery. Nothing but their Ignorance of our Numbers protects Us at this very time. When on the contrary, had We six or eight Thousand regular Troops, or could the

George Washington to the President of the Convention of New Hampshire, January 23, 1777
(The Gilder Lehrman Institute of American History, GLC00639.28, p. 1)

GEORGE WASHINGTON (1732–1799)

from Letter to the President of the Convention of New Hampshire, January 23, 1777

In autumn 1776, George Washington's army of fewer than 20,000 poorly trained and supplied troops nearly collapsed, retreating across New Jersey to Pennsylvania. On Christmas night, the Continental Army staged a surprise counterattack, crossing the Delaware River from Pennsylvania into New Jersey, and defeated the British forces at Trenton and, soon after, Princeton. These victories restored confidence in the American cause, but Washington still had to plead for additional troops and supplies from each of the individual states.

Headquart^{rs}. Morris Town. Jany. 23^{d}. 1777

The Situation to which I am reduced for want of a Regular body of Troops on whom I can depend for a length of time, makes it indispensably necessary for me to call upon You and intreat you to exert Yourselves in levying and equipping the number of Battalions allotted to your State by the Resolution of Congress in September last.

You must be fully sensible of the Hardship imposed upon Individuals, and how detrimental it must be to the Public, to have her Farmers and Tradesmen frequently called into the Field as Militia-men, whereby a total Stop is put to Arts & Agriculture, without which We can not possibly long subsist. But great as this Inconvenience is, We must put up with it, or submit to a greater, the total Loss of our Liberties, untill our regular Continental Army can be brought into the Field.

The above Reasons alone I hope will be Sufficient to induce you to exert Yourselves; for if our new Army are not ready to take the Field early in the Spring, We shall loose all the Advantages which I may say we have providentially gained this Winter. While our dependance is upon Militia, We have a full Army one day & Scarce any the next; And I am much afraid, that the Enemy one day or other, taking Advantage of one of these temporary Weaknesses, will make themselves Masters of our Magazines of Stores, Arms & Artillery. Nothing but their Ignorance of our Numbers protects Us at this very time. When on the contrary, had We six or eight Thousand regular Troops, or could the Militia, who were with me a few days ago, have been prevailed upon to Stay, We could have Struck such a Stroke, as would have inevitably ruined the Army of the Enemy in their divided State.

I am not without hopes, that by creating a powerfull Diversion on the side of New York, We may still keep their force divided between that Province & this; If so, and a good body of Regular troops could be thrown in to me before the Roads will be in a Condition for the Enemy with their reduced Waggon and Artillery horses, to move out, it perhaps may not be out of my power to Strike a decisive Blow before Spring – This is another and a forcible Reason to induce You to Send your new Levies forward with all Expedition. – While the men are raising, I beg you will spare no pains to make Collections of all things necessary for their Equipment; not only of Such as they carry with them into the Field, but for their Use and Convenience while they are there; such as Spare Shoes, Stockings & Shirts; the want of which has been the Ruin of the old Army. . . .

I am Y^{r}. mo. Ob. Hb Ser.

G^{o}: Washington

being long accustomed to command—will make you too haughty for mercantile matters—tho I hope you will not consider yourself as commander in chief of your own house—but be convinced tho not in the affair of Mr Coudray that there is such a thing as equal command—I send this by Capt Randal who says he expects to remain with you—pray how many of these lads have you—I am sure they must be very expensive—I am in want of some square dollars—which I expect from you to buy me a peice of linen an article I can do no longer without haveing had no recruit of that kind for almost five years girls in general when they marry are well stocked with these things but poor I had no such advantage——

Little Lucy who is without exception the sweetest child in the world—sends you a kiss—but where shall I take it from say you—from the paper I hope—but dare I say I sometimes fear that a long absence the force of bad example may lead you to forget me at some times—to know that it ever gave you pleasure to be in company with the finest woman in the world, would be worse than death to me—but it is not so, my Harry is too just too delicate too sincere, and too fond of his Lucy to admit the most remote thought of that distracting kind—away with it

dont be angry with me my Love—I am not jealous of your affection—I love you with a love as true and sacred as ever entered the human heart—but from a diffidence of my own merit I sometimes fear you will love me less after being so long from me—if you should may my life end before I know it—but I must die thinking you wholy mine—Adieu my love L K

Lucy Flucker Knox to Henry Knox, August 23, 1777
(The Gilder Lehrman Institute of American History, GLC02437.00638, p. 4)

LUCY FLUCKER KNOX (1756–1824)

from Letter to Henry Knox, August 23, 1777

The daughter of loyalists who had fled to England at the start of the Revolutionary War, Lucy Flucker Knox stayed in Boston when her husband, Henry, joined the Continental Army. In this letter, written on August 23, 1777, she discusses battlefield news, wartime profiteering, and family business and suggests that when General Knox returns home he should be willing to share "equal command" within the household.

Boston August 23rd 1777 –

My Dearest Friend –

. . . when I seriously reflect that I have lost my father Mother Brother and Sisters – intirely lost them – I am half distracted true I chearfully resigned them for one far dearer to me than all of them – but I am totaly deprived of him – I have not seen him for almost six months – and he writes me without pointing out any method by which I may ever expect to see him again – tis hard my Harry indeed it is I love you with the tenderest the purest affection – I would undergo any hardships to be near you and you will not lett me – suppose this campaign should be like the last carried into the winter – do you intend not to see me in all that time – tell me dear what your plan is. . . .

– oh that you had less of the military man about you – you might then after the war have lived at ease all the days of your life – but now I don't know what you will do – your being long acustomed to command – will make you too haughty for mercantile matters – tho I hope you will not consider yourself as commander in chief of your own house – but be convinced tho not in the affair of Mr Coudre that there is such a thing as equal command – I send this by Capt Randal who says he expects to remain with you – pray how many of these lads have have you – I am sure they must be very expensive – I am in want of some square dollars – which I expect from you to by me a peace of linen an article I can do no longer without haveing had no recruit of that kind for almost five years – girls in general when they marry are well stocked with those things but poor I had no such advantage –

little Lucy who is without exception the sweetest child in the world – sends you a kiss – but where shall I take it from say you – from the paper I hope – but dare I say I sometimes fear that a long absence the force of bad example may lead you to forget me at sometimes – to know that it ever gave you pleasure to be in company with the finest woman in the world, would be worse than death to me – but it is not so, my Harry is too just too delicate too sincere – and too fond of his Lucy to admit the most remote thought of that distracting kind – away with it – don't be angry with me my Love – I am not jealous of your affection – I love you with a love as true and sacred as ever entered the human heart – but from a diffidence of my own merit I sometimes fear you will Love me less – after being so long from me – if you should may my life end before I know it – that I may die thinking you wholly mine –

Adieu my love LK

York Town Feby 23. 1778.

My Honoured Father,

With much grief I received the account of your indisposition; but at the same time was happy to find you rather growing better, & that there was a prospect of your recovery. Not that I deemed you anxious to live; I supposed the contrary: but whether to live or die, I know you are perfectly resigned to the will of Heaven. — But for the sake of your family & friends, I wished you to live yet many years: that I too might again see you, & manifest that filial duty which I feel, & would cheerfully pay, to your latest breath.

When I look back on past time, I regret our difference of sentiment in great as well as (sometimes) in little politics; as it was a deduction from the happiness otherwise to have been enjoyed. Yet you had always too much regard to freedom in thinking & the rights of conscience, to lay upon me any injunctions which could interfere with my own opinion of what was my duty. In all things I have endeavoured to keep a good conscience, void of offence towards God and man. Often have I thanked my Maker for the greatest blessing of my

Timothy Pickering to Timothy Pickering Sr., February 23, 1778
(The Gilder Lehrman Institute of American History, GLC02325, p. 1)

TIMOTHY PICKERING (1745–1829)

Letter to Timothy Pickering Sr., February 23, 1778

In February 1778, Timothy Pickering Jr. received word from Massachusetts that his father was dying. An adjutant general in George Washington's Continental Army, Pickering wrote his father this moving letter of farewell on February 23, 1778. Pickering Jr. revered his father but disagreed with him on one critical issue: colonial independence from Great Britain. Pickering Jr. supported resistance to British rule, while Pickering Sr. remained a staunch Tory. The Revolution frequently divided families, but, as this letter indicates, the bonds of affection between Timothy Jr. and Sr. were never broken.

York Town Feby 23. 1778.

My Honoured Father,

With much grief I received the account of your indisposition; but at the same time was happy to find you rather growing better, & that there was a prospect of your recovery. Not that I deemed you anxious to live; I supposed the contrary: but whether to live or die, I know you are perfectly resigned to the will of Heaven.—But for the sake of your family & friends, I wished you to live yet many years: that I too might again see you, & manifest that filial duty which I feel, & would chearfully pay, to your latest breath.

When I look back on past time, I regret our difference of sentiment in great as well as (sometimes) in little politics; as it was a deduction from the happiness otherwise to have been enjoyed. Yet you had always too much regard to freedom in thinking & the rights of conscience, to lay upon me any injunctions which could interfere with my own opinion of what was my duty. In all things I have endeavoured to keep a good conscience, void of offence towards God and man. Often have I thanked my Maker for the greatest blessing of my life—your example & instructions in all the duties I owe to God, and my neighbour. They have not been lost upon me; tho' I am aware that in many things I have offended, & come short of my duty. For these things I am grieved; but not as those who have no hope.

I am deeply indebted too for your care in my education; I only regret that I improved my time no better.

But altho' the line of action I have pursued has not always been such as you would have chosen; yet (but I boast not) in regard to religion and morality, I hope you have never repented that I was your son. By God's grace I will in my future life aim at higher attainments in those all-essential points; not only from a sense of duty to my Creator—from a regard to my own happiness here and beyond the grave—but that I may never wound the breast of a parent to whom I am under so many and so great obligations.

My love and duty to you and my mother,

conclude me your obedient son,

Tim. Pickering junr:

.702

Gentlemen

I beg leave to state to you my necessitous circumstances, that through your intervention I may obtain that succour, which suffering humanity ever requires. Borne of African parents & as I apprehend in Boston, from whence while an infant I was removed to Rowley and from thence again to
Andover into the family of Doct. John Kiteredge, with whom,
as was then the lot of my unfortunate race, I passed the best
part of my life ~~as~~ a slave. ~~At the age of twentyfive~~ In the
year of our Lord 1775 or 6 & in the ~~twentyfifth~~ of my age I entered into the service of the U.S. as a private soldier ~~where~~ I continued five years and where I contracted a complaint from which
I have suffered in a greater or less degree ever since &
with which I am now afflicted. After leaving the army I
became a sailor for five years; when I quited the sea & resided
for some time in Newtown, from whence I went to Natick where I remained for a short time & then removed
to Dover where I [carried] ~~remained~~ on as a day labourer during the
period of seven years. Eight years past I removed to the place
where I now live, & have untill this time, by my labour,
assisted by the kindness of the neighbouring inhabitants been
enabled to support myself and family. At present having arrived

Peter Kiteredge to the Selectmen of Medfield, Massachusetts, April 26, 1806
(The Gilder Lehrman Institute of American History, GLC01450.702, p. 1)

PETER KITEREDGE (fl. 1775–1806)

Petition to the Selectmen of Medfield, Massachusetts, April 26, 1806

Born into slavery in Massachusetts, Peter Kiteredge entered the military when he was twenty-five and served in the American Revolution for five years. Afterward, he spent time as a sailor and a laborer. Due to an illness that left him disabled, Kiteredge requested assistance from Medfield officials to support his wife and four children, fearing that he could no longer earn a living.

Gentlemen

I beg leave to state to you my necessitious circumstances, that through your intervention I may obtain that succour, which suffering humanity ever requires. Borne of African parents & as I apprehend in Boston, from whence while an infant I was removed to Rowley and from thence again to Andover into the family of Doct. Thom Kiteridge, with whom, as was then the lot of my unfortunate race, I passed the best part of my life as a slave. In the year of our Lord 1775 or 6 & in the twenty fifth of my age I entered into the servise of the U.S. as a private soldier where I continued five years and where I contracted a complaint from which I have suffered in a greater or less degree ever since & with which I am now afflicted. After leaving the army to become a sailor for two years; when I quited the sea & resided for some time in Newtown, from whence I went to Natick where I remained for a short time & then removed to Dover where I tarried as a day labourer during the period of seven years. Eight years past I removed to the place where I now live, & have untill this time, by my labor, assisted by the kindness of the neighbouring inhabitants been enabled to support myself and family. At present having arrived at the fifty eight year of my life and afflicted with severe and as I apprehend with incurable diseases whereby the labour of my hands is wholly cut off, and with it the only means of my support.—My family at this time consists of a wife and four children, three of whome are so young as to be unable to support themselves and the time of their mother is wholy occupied in taking cair of myself & our little ones – Thus gentlemen, in this my extremity I am induced to call on you for assistance; not in the character of an inhabitant of the town of Medfield, for I have no such claim. but as a stranger accidently fallen within your borders, one who has not the means of subsistence, & in fact, one, who must fail through want & disease unless sustained by the fostering hand of your care.

I am Gentlemen your mos obedient, most humble servant.

Peter Kiteredge
His X Mark

Attest. Ebenezer Clark
Paul Hither

Section III

CREATING THE CONSTITUTION

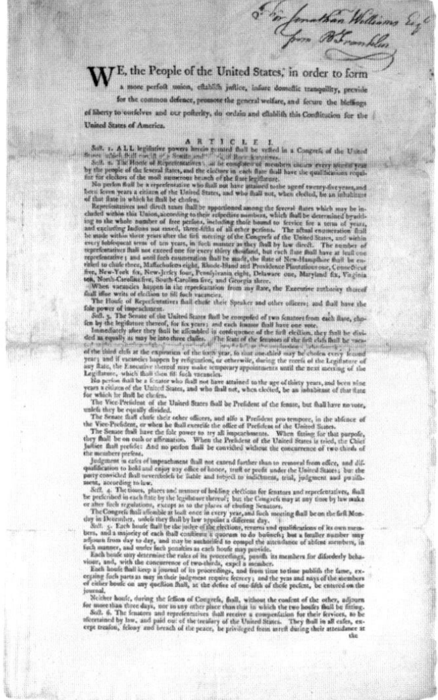

To Jonathan Williams Esq.
from B. Franklin

WE, the People of the United States, in order to form a more perfect union, establish justice, insure domestic tranquility, provide for the common defence, promote the general welfare, and secure the blessings of liberty to ourselves and our posterity, do ordain and establish this Constitution for the United States of America.

ARTICLE I.

Final draft of the US Constitution, inscribed by Benjamin Franklin, September 17, 1787
(The Gilder Lehrman Institute of American History, GLC03585, p. 1)

Section III

Creating the Constitution

by Carol Berkin

DOCUMENTS

- *from* The Articles of Confederation, 1777
- *from* George Washington, Circular letter to the states, addressed to William Livingston, June 12, 1783
- *from* George Washington to Henry Knox, April 2, 1787
- *from* Mercy Otis Warren to Catharine Macaulay, September 28, 1787
- *from* Henry Knox to the Marquis de Lafayette, October 24, 1787

A. OVERVIEW

From 1776 to 1783, American colonists waged a long war for independence from Great Britain. During that war, the colonies became independent sovereign states and each of them wrote a constitution describing the structure of their governments and, in many cases, stating the rights and liberties of their citizens. These states agreed to form a "league of friendship," a confederation that would be empowered to wage war and make peace, but leave taxation and trade regulations and other vital functions to the control of the states themselves. Thus the first American constitution, the Articles of Confederation, did not create a unified nation, and soon proved to be too restricted in authority to deal with many of the crises and problems that emerged after independence.

B. THEMES

1. The Limitations of the Confederation's Powers

Although some historians refer to the Articles of Confederation as "weak," it is better to think of them as "limited." The desire to keep power close to home, that is, in the hands of the states rather than a distant central government, is understandable considering that the Americans were in the midst of fighting a war against a government in London. Yet men like Alexander Hamilton, James Madison, and George Washington soon came to believe that what they called an "energetic government" would better protect the new nation.

2. American Crises and the Making of "a More Perfect Union"

We often forget that every generation of Americans has experienced major crises. The years between the winning of independence and the ratification of the Constitution have, in fact, been called "the critical period in American history." In his circular letter to the states in June 1783, George Washington emphasized how anxious political leaders were about the fate of the young nation after the achievement of "absolute Freedom and Independency."

By 1787, Washington, Hamilton, and Madison began to worry that the fragile American experiment in representative government might fail. This is why, along with fifty-two other men, they gathered in Philadelphia to design a new constitution that would, in fact, create a nation.

The mood of this Philadelphia convention was somber. Most of the planters, lawyers, and merchants who attended had been driven by a fear that their country might be picked apart and swallowed up by the European titans, or driven back from the Ohio Valley by American Indians—or worst of all, that it would collapse on its own, weighted down by embarrassing debt accrued during the Revolution, by commercial feuds among the states, by conflicts between farmers and urban merchants, or by uprisings of enslaved people. Even Hamilton, the most visionary of these eighteenth-century political leaders, could not imagine the global power, the productivity and prosperity, or the democratic ethos we sometimes take for granted today.

The Constitution these delegates produced drew on principles and practices familiar to most Americans then and today. It was based firmly on a belief in the rule of law, not of men. Unlike the Articles of Confederation, it gave the government a broad range of powers, including the power to tax, to regulate commerce, and to create a uniform currency. In its form, it was based upon the separation of powers among judicial, legislative, and executive branches already established by the English government, the delegates' own colonial governments, and the new state governments. But this Constitution was distinguished by two major political innovations. The first was the assertion that the government's power, or sovereignty, arose from the citizens themselves; the second was the idea of federalism. The assertion that the citizens were sovereign meant America would be a republic with a representative government. This made it unique in the eighteenth century until the French Revolution. Federalism was equally remarkable, for it was a system that divided sovereignty and authority between two levels of government—the states and the federal government. This was something most European countries considered too radical to succeed. Under federalism, some powers belonged exclusively to the national government, some powers belonged exclusively to the state governments, and some powers belonged to both. The adoption of this system soon led to arguments over where ultimate authority resided, and these arguments have been a major part of our national history right up until today.

3. To Ratify or Not to Ratify the Constitution

Although the men who wrote the Constitution met in secret, they had no intention of staging a coup d'état. They would not impose their will on the American citizens with swords or guns. Instead they submitted their Constitution to the judgment of the voters. For some, the choice to ratify or not to ratify was a difficult one. On September 28, 1787, one vocal critic, Mercy Otis Warren, expressed her objections to the new form of government: "[W]e have struggled for liberty & made lofty sacrifices at her shrine: and there are still many among us who revere her name too much to relinquish (beyond a certain medium) the rights of man for the Dignity of Government." Some weeks later, on October 24, Henry Knox wrote to the Marquis de Lafayette that the very future of the nation was in the balance: "[The] propositions . . . are contemplated by the public at large with an anxious attention. The discussions are commenced in the newspapers & in Phampletts, with all the freedom & liberality which characterize a people who are searching by their own experience after a form of government most productive of happiness."

In each state, ratifying conventions met to debate replacing the Articles with the new, "energetic" form of government. At these conventions, the Federalists who supported ratification and the Anti-federalists who opposed it engaged in intense argument. Anti-federalists voiced a widely held view that the proposed new government was too powerful, that it concentrated too much power in the hands of a small and elite group of men, and thus it would inevitably become a tyranny. Anti-federalists pointed to the absence of a bill of rights in the proposed constitution as proof that it could easily devolve into tyranny. The liberties and rights of the people, they said, were better protected by state governments made up of local men who shared the interests of those who elected them. The Federalists responded to these charges. In their most famous series of essays, the Federalist Papers, three Federalists—James Madison, Alexander Hamilton, and John Jay—argued, among other things, that the checks and balances built into the Constitution as well as the sheer size and variety of economic interests of the country would protect against the rise of a tyrant or the emergence of an oligarchy. In the end, the Federalists carried the day. Rhode Island and North Carolina, however, refused to join the Union until after the Bill of Rights was submitted to the states. In 1789, the first Federal Congress met in New York City and the first President, George Washington, took the oath of office.

C. QUESTIONS

1. If a new constitutional convention were called in your lifetime, what issues do you believe would be on the agenda and which would be the most controversial?
2. Is federalism still a source of conflict and tension within American politics? What contemporary issues raise problems between the states and the federal government? What solutions would you propose?
3. In the eighteenth century, political debate took place in pamphlets, newspapers, and often in taverns. Where do these debates take place today—and what are the strengths and weaknesses of these modern forums?

ARTICLES

OF

CONFEDERATION

AND

PERPETUAL UNION

BETWEEN THE

STATES

OF

NEW-HAMPSHIRE, MASSACHUSETTS-BAY, RHODE-ISLAND AND PROVIDENCE PLANTATIONS, CONNECTICUT, NEW-YORK, NEW-JERSEY, PENNSYLVANIA, DELAWARE, MARY-LAND, VIRGINIA, NORTH-CAROLINA, SOUTH-CAROLINA AND GEORGIA.

LANCASTER, (PENNSYLVANIA,) PRINTED:

BOSTON, RE-PRINTED BY JOHN GILL, PRINTER TO THE GENERAL ASSEMBLY.
M,DCC,LXXVII.

The Articles of Confederation, 1777
(The Gilder Lehrman Institute of American History, GLC00268, p. 1)

from THE ARTICLES OF CONFEDERATION (1777)

In 1781, the thirteen original states ratified America's first national system of government, the Articles of Confederation. The Articles represented an attempt to balance the sovereignty of the states with an effective national government. As the primary organ of the national government, Congress had the power to declare war, appoint military officers, sign treaties, and make alliances. Under the Articles, the states, not Congress, had the power to tax. In addition, Congress could not draft soldiers or regulate trade. There was no provision for national courts or a chief executive. The Articles served as the nation's plan of government until the Constitution went into effect in 1789.

ARTICLES

Of Confederation and perpetual Union between the States of *New-Hampshire, Massachusetts-Bay, Rhode-Island* and *Providence Plantations, Connecticut, New-York, New-Jersey, Pennsylvania, Delaware, Maryland, Virginia, North-Carolina, South-Carolina* and *Georgia.*

ART. V. [Manner of constituting the Congress of the States, with the qualifications & privileges of the delegates.]

For the more convenient management of the general interests of the United States, delegates shall be annually appointed in such manner as the legislature of each state shall direct, to meet in Congress on the first Monday in November, in every year, with a power reserved to each state, to recal its delegates, or any of them, at any time within the year, and to send others in their stead for the remainder of the year.

No state shall be represented in Congress by less than two, nor by more than seven members; and no person shall be capable of being a delegate for more than three years, in any term of six years; nor shall any person, being a delegate, be capable of holding any office under the United States, for which he, or another for his benefit receives any salary, fees or emolument of any kind.

Each state shall maintain its own delegates in a meeting of the states, and while they act as members of the committee of the states.

In determining questions in the United States, in Congress assembled, each state shall have one vote.

Freedom of speech and debate in Congress shall not be impeached or questioned in any court, or place out of Congress, and the members of Congress shall be protected in their persons from arrests and imprisonments, during the time of their going to and from, and attendance on Congress, except for treason, felony, or breach of the peace.

[Circular]

Head Quarters Newburgh
June 12th 1783—

Sir

The great object for which I had the honor to hold an Appointment in the Service of my Country being accomplished, I am now preparing to resign it into the hands of Congress, and to return to that domestic retirement which it is well known I left with the greatest reluctance; a Retirement for which I have never ceased to sigh through a long and painfull absence; and in which (remote from the noise & trouble of the World) I meditate to pass the remainder of life, in a state of undisturbed repose; — But before I carry this resolution into effect, I think it a duty incumbent on me, to make this my last official communication, to congratulate you on the glorious events which Heaven has been pleased to produce in our favor, to offer my sentiments respecting some important subjects, which appear to me to be intimately connected with the tranquility of the United States, to take my leave of your Excellency as a public Character, and to give my final blessing to that Country, in whose service I have spent

George Washington, Circular letter to the states, addressed to William Livingston, June 12, 1783 (The Gilder Lehrman Institute of American History, GLC08079, p. 1)

GEORGE WASHINGTON (1732–1799)

from Circular letter to the states, addressed to William Livingston, June 12, 1783

Upon his retirement from military command at the end of the American Revolution, George Washington drafted a set of principles for the survival of the new nation. Sent to William Livingston of New Jersey and other state governors, Washington's circular letter addresses a critical moment when Americans would either "establish or ruin their national Character forever," watched by "the Eyes of the whole World."

The Citizens of America, placed in the most enviable condition, as the sole Lords and Proprietors of a vast tract of Continent, comprehending all the various soils and climates of the World, and abounding with all the necessaries and conveniences of life, are now, by the late satisfactory pacification, acknowledged to be possessed of absolute freedom and Independency. They are from this period to be considered as the Actors on a most conspicuous theatre, which seems to be peculiarly designated by Providence for the display of human greatness and felicity. Here they are not only surrounded with every thing which can contribute to the completion of private and domestic enjoyment, but Heaven has crowned all its other blessings, by giving a fairer opportunity for political happiness, than any other Nation has ever been favored with. –Nothing can illustrate these observations more forcibly, than a recollection of the happy conjuncture of times and circumstances, under which our Republic assumed its rank among the Nations. The foundation of our Empire was not laid in the gloomy Age of ignorance and superstition, but at an Epocha when the rights of Mankind were better understood, and more clearly defined than at any former period, the researches of the human mind after social happiness, have been carried to a great extent, the Treasures of knowledge acquired by the labours of Philosophers, Sages and Legislators through a long succession of years, are laid open for our use, and their collected wisdom may be happily applied in the establishment of our forms of Government, the free cultivation of Letters, the unbounded extension of Commerce, the progressive refinement of manners, the growing liberality of sentiment, and above all the pure and benign light of Revelation, have had a meliorating influence on mankind, and increased the blessings of Society. At this auspicious period, the United States came into existence as a Nation, and if the Citizens should not be completely free and happy, the fault will be entirely their own.

Such is our situation, and such are our prospects: but notwithstanding the cup of blessing is thus reached out to us, notwithstanding happiness is ours if we have a disposition to seize the occasion & make it our own; yet, it appears to me there is an option still left to the United States of America, that it is in their choice, and depends upon their conduct, whether they will be respectable and prosperous, or contemptable and miserable as a Nation — This is the time of their political probation — this is the moment when the Eyes of the whole World are turned upon them — this is the moment to establish or ruin their national Character forever — this is the favorable moment to give such a tone to our Fœderal Government as will enable it to answer the ends of its institution — or this may be the ill-fated moment for relaxing the powers of the Union, annihilating the cement of the Confederation, and exposing us to become the sport of European Politics, which may play one State against another to prevent their growing importance, and to serve their own interested purposes: — for according to the System of Policy the States shall adopt at this moment, they will stand or fall, and by their confirmation or lapse it is yet to be decided, whether the Revolution must Ultimately be considered as a blessing or a curse: a blessing or a curse, not to the present age alone, for with our fate will the destiny of unborn Millions be involved.

(27) LIII-67 3782

Mount Vernon 2. Apr. 1787.

My dear Sir,

The early attention which you were so obliging as to pay to my letter of the 8th ult. is highly pleasing and flattering to me.—Were you to continue to give me information on the same point you would add to the favor; as I see, or think I see, reasons for and against my attendance in Convention so near an equilibrium, as will cause me to determine upon either with diffidence.—One of the reasons against it is, an apprehension that all the States will not appear; and that some of them, being unwillingly drawn into the measure, will send their Delegates so fettered as to embarrass & perhaps render nugatory the whole proceedings.—In either of these circumstances—that is a partial representation—or cramped powers, I should not like to be a sharer in this business.—If the Delegates come with such powers—as

George Washington to Henry Knox, April 2, 1787
(The Gilder Lehrman Institute of American History, GLC02437.09412, p. 1)

GEORGE WASHINGTON (1732–1799)

from Letter to Henry Knox, April 2, 1787

Writing to his Revolutionary War comrade Henry Knox, Washington gives his reasons for not wanting to attend the Constitutional Convention, including the possibility that certain states might not attend, rendering representation partial. In Washington's view, the Convention would be a success only if all delegates attended and used their authority to correct the flaws of the Articles of Confederation.

Mount Vernon 2d. Aprl. 1787.

My dear Sir;

The early attention which you were so obliging as to pay to my letter of the 8th. ulto. is highly pleasing and flattering to me. – Were you to continue to give me information on the same point, you would add to the favor; as I see, or think I see, reasons for and against my attendance in Convention so near an equilibrium, as will cause me to Determine upon either, with diffidence. – One of the reasons against it, is, an apprehension that all the States will not appear; and that some of them, being unwillingly drawn into the measure, will send their Delegates so fettered as to embarrass, & perhaps render nugatory, the whole proceedings. – In either of these circumstances, – that is – a partial representation – or cramped powers, I should not like to be a sharer in this business. – If the Delegates come with such powers as will enable the Convention to probe the defects of the Constitution to the bottom, and point out radical cures – it would be an honorable employment – but otherwise it is desireable to avoid it and these are matters you may possibly come at by means of your acquaintances among the Delegates in Congress; who, undoubtedly know what powers are given by their respective States. –You also can inform me what the prevailing opinion with respect to my attendance, or non-attendance, is; – and I would sincerely thank you for the confidential communication of it.

Milton Sept 28 1787

I have my dear Madam postponed writing by several opportunities as I wished for the pleasure of transmitting to you the result of the Grand Convention of the united States. every thing has for some time hung suspended on their determinations. I now forward them to you without any comment thereon. first because I do not think myself qualified to make any. and in the next place it might not be thought altogether prudent. It is now only three days since the publication of the recommendations of this respectable body has appeared in our papers. almost every one whom I have yet seen read, with attention holds the page with solemnity & silently wraps up his opinion within his own breast, as if afraid of interrupting that calm expectation that has pervaded all ranks for several months past.

Our situation is truly delicate & critical. on the one hand we

Mercy Otis Warren to Catharine Macaulay, September 28, 1787
(The Gilder Lehrman Institute of American History, GLC01800.03, p. 1)

MERCY OTIS WARREN (1728–1814)

from Letter to Catharine Macaulay, September 28, 1787

Mercy Otis Warren wrote this letter to her English correspondent Catharine Macaulay three days after the Constitution was adopted in Philadelphia. Regardless of individual reactions to the Constitution, she notes, everyone seems conscious of its importance. In September 1787 the question of ratification was, in Warren's words, "truly delicate & critical."

Milton Sept 28 1787

I have my dear Madam postponed writing by several opportunities as I wished for the pleasure of transmiting to you the result of the Grand Convention of the United States. every thing has for some time hung suspended in their determinations. I now forward them to you without any comment thereon. just because I do not think myself qualified to make any: and in the next place it might not be thought altogether prudent.

It is now only three days since the publication of the recommendations of this respectable body has appeared in our papers. almost every one whom I have yet seen reads with attention holds the page with solemnity & silently wraps up his opinion within his own breast, as if affraid of interrupting that calm expectation that has pervaded all ranks for several months past.

Our situation is truly delicate & critical. on the one hand we stand in need of a strong Federal Government founded on principles that will support the prosperity & union of the colonies. on the other we have struggled for liberty & made lofty sacrifices at her shrine: and there are still many among us who revere her name too much to relinquish (beyond a certain medium) the rights of man for the Dignity of Government.

I should be happy to hear the observations of a Lady (who has made politics & Government so much the subject of her contemplations) on this new and complicated system; which I suppose will set in motion both the pens & the tongues of the political world.

Happy indeed will this Country be if a tranquil energetic Government can be adopted before the sword is drawn to give it a despotic master.

HK. To Lafayette

783 693 XXI-27

To Lafayette 1787

New-York 24 October 1787

My dear Marquis

You will have received long before this period, the ~~proceedings~~ result of the Convention which assembled in Philadelphia during the month of May— These propositions being essentially different, in many respects from the existing Confederation, and which will probably produce different national effects, are contemplated by the public at large with an anxious attention. The discussions are commenced in the news papers & in Phamphletts, with all the freedom & liberality which characterize a people who are searching by their own experience after a form, of government most productive of happiness—

Henry Knox to the Marquis de Lafayette, October 24, 1787
(The Gilder Lehrman Institute of American History, GLC02437.03680, p. 1)

HENRY KNOX (1750–1806)

from Letter to the Marquis de Lafayette, October 24, 1787

In this letter to the Marquis de Lafayette, Continental Army veteran Henry Knox expresses his approval of a stronger national government and his certainty that the Constitution will provide it. While he acknowledges that the Constitution is not a perfect document, finding "several things in it that I confess I could wish to be altered," he asserts that the American people are ready for the change it brings.

New-York 24 October 1787

My dear Marquis

You will have received long before this period, the results of the Convention which assembled in Philadelphia during the month of May – These propositions being essentially different, in many respects from the existing confederation, and which will probably produce different national effects, are contemplated by the public at large with an anxious attention. The discussions are commenced in the newspapers & in Phampletts, with all the freedom & liberality which characterize a people who are searching by their own experience after a form, of government most productive of happiness –

To speak decisively at this moment of the fate of the proposed constitution characterizes effectively the person, giving the opinion – [Habited as] I have been for a long period to desire the consolodation of the powers of all parts of this country as an indispensible [*illegible*] to a national character & national happiness I receive the propositions as they are and from my soul I wish them God speed. The transition from, wishing an event to beleiving that it will happen is easy indeed – perhaps I therefore am led in to a strong persuasion that the proposed government will be generally or universally adopted in the course of twelve or fifteen months –

In desiring that the proposed government may be adopted I would [not] that you should beleive that I think it all perfect. There are several things in it that I confess I could wish to be altered. But I apprehend no alterations can be effected peaceably. All the states represented agreed to the constitution as it stands. There are substantial reasons to beleive that such an agreement could not again be produced even by the same men – the minds of the people at large were fully prepared for a change without any particular specification – The proposition will be discussed fully – [parties] will be raised – were therefore the same work to be again discussed the Representatives of the different States would repair to the convention with instructions, respecting their assent unless certain powers [favord] to the interest of the particular States should be established. Hence it would result, that no agreemt could be made which depended on [such] a mutual accomodation. This single circumstance, independent of the connections which might & probably would arise in the interim is sufficient of itself to point out the importance and value of the new Constitution.

Section IV

GOVERNING THE NEW NATION

Alexander Hamilton, ca. 1800
(The Gilder Lehrman Institute of American History, GLC08343)

Section IV

Governing the New Nation

by Julie Silverbrook

DOCUMENTS

- Preamble to the first draft of the US Constitution, August 6, 1787, and Preamble to the final draft of the US Constitution, September 17, 1787
- from *Report . . . [on] the Public Credit* by Alexander Hamilton, 1790
- *from* George Washington to Jonathan Trumbull, July 21, 1799
- *from* Alexander Hamilton to Harrison Gray Otis, December 23, 1800
- from *Communications from Several States, on the Resolutions of the Legislature of Virginia, Respecting the Alien & Sedition Laws*, 1800

A. OVERVIEW

The US Constitution was signed on September 17, 1787. The final document represents a significant transformation of the nature of the nation from a collection of states to a union. The document was ratified on June 21, 1788, and went into effect on March 4, 1789, a month after George Washington was unanimously elected as President of the United States. On April 30, 1789, Washington took the presidential oath of office at Federal Hall in New York City. In his first inaugural address, he described what was at stake as government began under the new Constitution: "The preservation of the sacred fire of liberty, and the destiny of the republican model of government, are justly considered as *deeply*, perhaps as *finally* staked, on the experiment entrusted to the hands of the American people."

However, the success of the American experiment in constitutional government was by no means assured. In fact, the first decade of government under the new Constitution was a turbulent and fragile one, filled with uncertainty, discord, and foreign threats. For example, the nation faced staggering foreign and domestic debts that threatened to tear the new national government apart. To deal with these, Alexander Hamilton, the nation's first treasury secretary, formulated an ambitious economic program to repay American debts, attract foreign investors, create a national bank, and aid the nation's new manufacturing industries. Hamilton's program was a huge success, but intense negotiations and political compromises were necessary to overcome opposition to his proposals, especially from the agrarian South.

B. THEMES

1. Establishing a National Economy

Throughout US history, Americans have debated how best to manage government debts. In his *Report [on] Public Credit* (1790), Treasury Secretary Alexander Hamilton proposed the assumption by the federal government of outstanding state debts from the Revolutionary War. States including Pennsylvania, North Carolina, Maryland, and Virginia, which had already paid off their debts, opposed paying taxes to wipe out other states' debts. For six months, a bitter debate raged in Congress. A compromise settled the issue: southern leaders would support Hamilton's plan if the Washington administration agreed to locate the new national capital on the banks of the Potomac River between Virginia and Maryland. By demonstrating Americans' willingness to repay their debts, Hamilton made the United States attractive to foreign investors, and European investment capital began pouring into the country.

Hamilton also won a victory in the battle over creating a Bank of the United States. Jefferson and Madison argued that establishing a bank exceeded the powers expressly granted to the federal government by the Constitution. By appealing to the "Necessary and Proper" clause in Article One of the Constitution, Hamilton effectively made his case. Congress ultimately supported Hamilton's position and in 1791, the first Bank of the United States was granted a twenty-year charter.

Hamilton's only major defeat was in his effort to see the federal government actively encourage manufacturing. Thomas Jefferson effectively challenged Hamilton's plan to develop industry, believing that it too strongly favored northeastern interests over those of the South. Jefferson also argued that it threatened the country's agrarian way of life, which he viewed as instrumental to the preservation of liberty.

2. Dissent and National Security

In 1796, President Washington warned Americans against foreign entanglements in his farewell address, and yet the new nation found itself in a "quasi war" with France after the European power insulted American diplomats in what came to be known as the XYZ Affair of 1798. Anxieties about foreign influence exacerbated domestic conflicts as well.

In the late 1790s, President John Adams and the Federalists who controlled Congress considered the harsh criticism of Federalist policies by Thomas Jefferson's opposition party, the Democratic-Republicans, as a sign of disloyalty to the Constitution and the US government. They feared that the opposition party was growing stronger due to support from immigrants to the United States. Concerned that these foreigners would sympathize with the French in the 1798 conflict, Congress passed four laws, known collectively as the Alien and Sedition Acts.

The Alien and Sedition Acts suppressed criticism of the government and led Thomas Jefferson and James Madison to author resolutions adopted by the Kentucky and Virginia legislatures. In these resolutions, Jefferson and Madison argued that the Alien and Sedition Acts were unconstitutional and could be subject to nullification by the states. The doctrines of states' rights and nullification later threatened to tear the nation apart over the issues of tariffs and slavery.

3. The Presidential Election of 1800 and the Peaceful Transition of Power

The political backlash against the Alien and Sedition Acts was one factor contributing to the electoral defeat of the Federalists in the presidential election of 1800. This election, between incumbent John Adams and his vice president, Thomas Jefferson, was divisive and dirty, and seemed to threaten the nation's very survival. The bitter partisan contest revealed a constitutional defect: under the Constitution, votes for president and vice president were not listed on separate ballots, and Jefferson and his running mate Aaron Burr received the same number of electoral votes. In a letter of December 1800 to Massachusetts representative Harrison Gray Otis, Alexander Hamilton expressed unequivocal support for his longtime political opponent Jefferson, writing that he was, unlike the power-hungry Burr, "a lover of liberty [who] will be desirous of something like orderly Government." After thirty-five failed ballots, the House of Representatives finally selected Jefferson as the next president of the United States. Jefferson's election and the Federalist defeat in Congress marked the first time the government under the new Constitution changed party hands. To remedy the problem of a tie between a candidate and his running mate, the Twelfth Amendment was passed and ratified in 1804. The most significant thing about the election of 1800, however, was that it represented a peaceful transition of political power from one party to another.

Despite the turbulence of the first decade of government under the Constitution, the decisions of the first Congresses and presidential elections ensured the new nation's survival.

C. QUESTIONS

1. Madison and Jefferson opposed the Alien and Sedition Acts, which suppressed dissent and freedom of the press, as unconstitutional. With the balance between preserving free speech and maintaining national security in today's headlines, how do Americans shape debates about dissent and freedom of the individual as set forth in the First Amendment?
2. Since the founding, supporters of the federal government's authority have clashed with defenders of states' rights, who have asserted the right to overturn laws not stipulated by the Constitution. Where does the ultimate power of the American people reside, with the federal government or with the individual states?
3. The election of 1800 highlighted a flaw in the procedures for electing a president. Jefferson and Burr appeared on the same ballot and received equal votes, because the Electoral College had no clear guidelines for breaking a tie. Today, concerns over the Electoral College focus on a different issue: that a presidential candidate can win in the Electoral College but lose the national popular vote. Do we need the Electoral College today?

THE CONSTITUTION OF THE UNITED STATES (1787)

Preamble to the first draft of the US Constitution, August 6, 1787

Printed as the basis for the delegates' deliberations at the Constitutional Convention in August 1787, this copy of the first draft of the Constitution was owned by Pierce Butler, a delegate from South Carolina, whose handwritten notes and emendations are visible throughout. The preambles to the draft—"We the People of the States of . . ."—and to the final version—"We, the People of the United States"—show that in the six weeks between the writing of the draft and of the final version the idea of a united nation had been born.

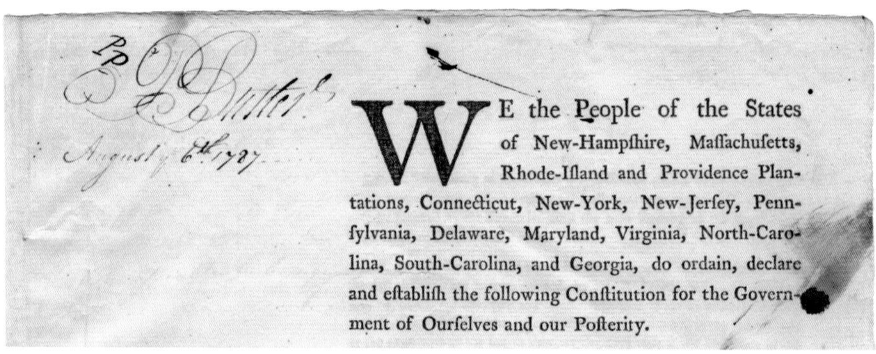

WE the People of the States of New-Hampſhire, Maſſachuſetts, Rhode-Iſland and Providence Plantations, Connecticut, New-York, New-Jerſey, Pennſylvania, Delaware, Maryland, Virginia, North-Carolina, South-Carolina, and Georgia, do ordain, declare and eſtabliſh the following Conſtitution for the Government of Ourſelves and our Poſterity.

Preamble to the first draft of the US Constitution, August 6, 1787
(The Gilder Lehrman Institute of American History, GLC00819.01)

Preamble to the final draft of the US Constitution, inscribed by Benjamin Franklin, September 17, 1787

The final text of the Constitution was printed on September 17, 1787, and distributed to the delegates, among whom Benjamin Franklin, aged eighty-one, was the senior member. Franklin signed this copy as a gift for his nephew Jonathan Williams.

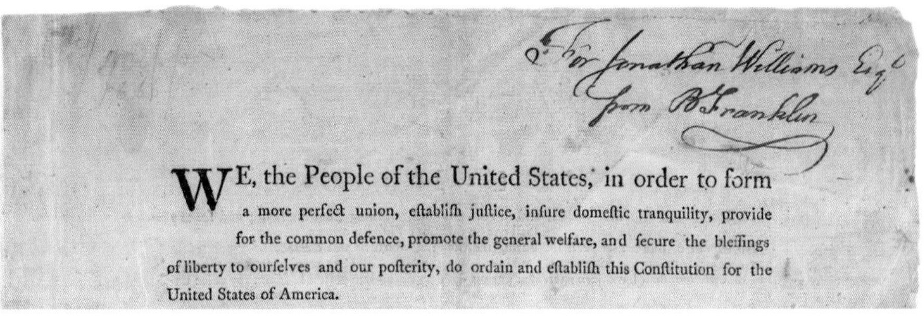

For Jonathan Williams Esqr
from B Franklin

WE, the People of the United States, in order to form a more perfect union, eſtabliſh juſtice, inſure domeſtic tranquility, provide for the common defence, promote the general welfare, and ſecure the bleſſings of liberty to ourſelves and our poſterity, do ordain and eſtabliſh this Conſtitution for the United States of America.

Preamble to the final draft of the US Constitution, inscribed by Benjamin Franklin to Jonathan Williams, printed by Dunlap & Claypoole, September 17, 1787
(The Gilder Lehrman Institute of American History, GLC03585)

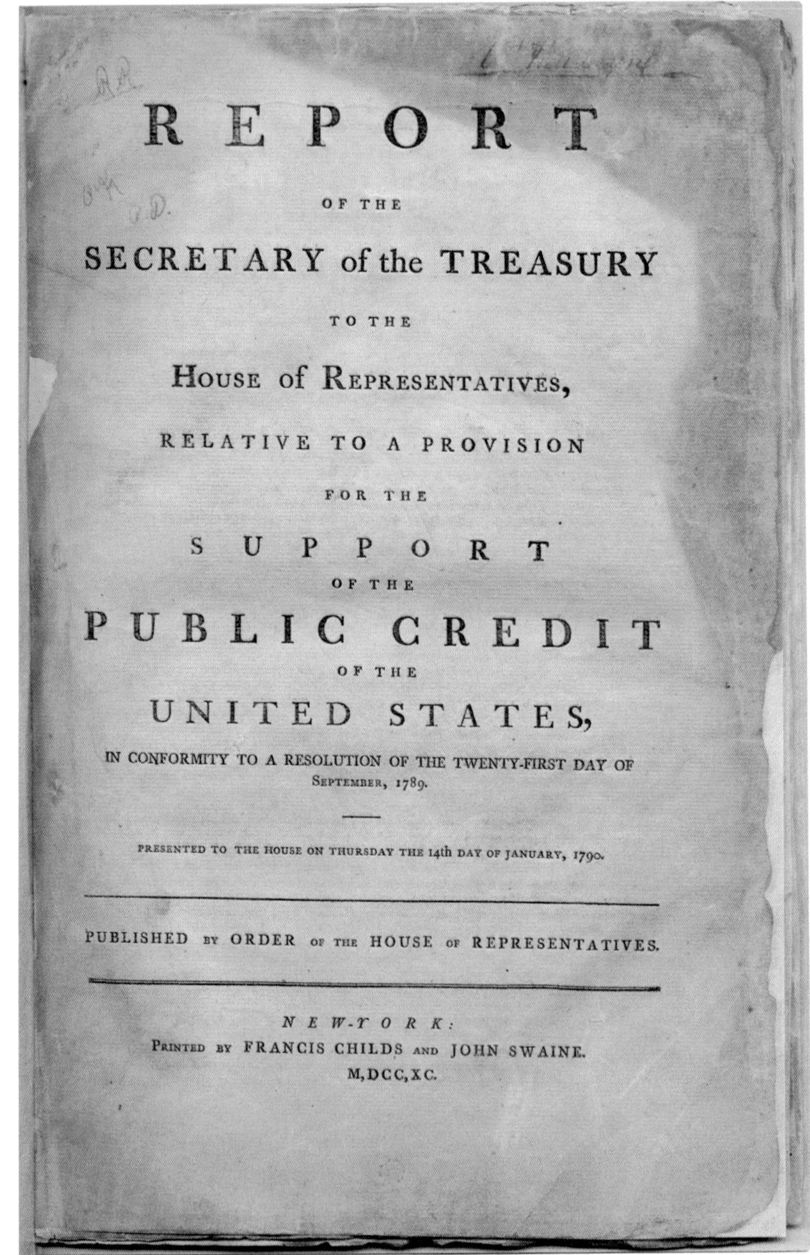

REPORT

OF THE

SECRETARY of the TREASURY

TO THE

HOUSE of REPRESENTATIVES,

RELATIVE TO A PROVISION

FOR THE

SUPPORT

OF THE

PUBLIC CREDIT

OF THE

UNITED STATES,

IN CONFORMITY TO A RESOLUTION OF THE TWENTY-FIRST DAY OF SEPTEMBER, 1789.

PRESENTED TO THE HOUSE ON THURSDAY THE 14th DAY OF JANUARY, 1790.

PUBLISHED BY ORDER OF THE HOUSE OF REPRESENTATIVES.

NEW-YORK:
PRINTED BY FRANCIS CHILDS AND JOHN SWAINE.
M,DCC,XC.

Report of the Secretary of the Treasury to the House of Representatives, Relative to a Provision for the Support of the Public Credit of the United States by Alexander Hamilton, 1790
(The Gilder Lehrman Institute of American History, GLC00960)

ALEXANDER HAMILTON (ca. 1757–1804)

from *Report . . . [on] the Public Credit* (New York, 1790), p. 4.

Appointed by President Washington to be the first treasury secretary in 1789, Alexander Hamilton pushed a stream of reports, acts, and institutions through Congress to create a firm fiscal foundation for the new nation. Among his first measures, as proposed in his *Report. . . [on] Public Credit* (1790), was the federal assumption of state debts, a radical plan that would both establish a sound credit rating internationally and tie individual debtors to the success of the federal, rather than state, government.

While the observance of that good faith, which is the basis of public credit, is recommended by the strongest inducements of political expediency, it is enforced by considerations of still greater authority. There are arguments for it, which rest on the immutable principles of moral obligation. And in proportion as the mind is disposed to contemplate, in the order of Providence, an intimate connection between public virtue and public happiness, will be its repugnancy to a violation of those principles.

This reflection derives additional strength from the nature of the debt of the United States. It was the price of liberty. The faith of America has been repeatedly pledged for it, and with solemnities, that give peculiar force to the obligation. There is indeed reason to regret that it has not hitherto been kept; that the necessities of the war, conspiring with inexperience in the subjects of finance, produced direct infractions; and that the subsequent period has been a continued scene of negative violation, or non-compliance. But a diminution of this regret arises from the reflection, that the last seven years have exhibited an earnest and uniform effort, on the part of the government of the union, to retrieve the national credit, by doing justice to the creditors of the nation; and that the embarrassments of a defective constitution, which defeated this laudable effort, have ceased.

From this evidence of a favorable disposition, given by the former government, the institution of a new one, cloathed with powers competent to calling forth the resources of the community, has excited correspondent expectations. A general belief, accordingly, prevails, that the credit of the United States will quickly be established on the firm foundation of an effectual provision for the existing debt. The influence, which this has had at home, is witnessed by the rapid increase, that has taken place in the market value of the public securities. From January to November, they rose thirty-three and a third per cent, and from that period to this time, they have risen fifty per cent more. And the intelligence from abroad announces effects proportionably favourable to our national credit and consequence.

It cannot but merit particular attention, that among ourselves the most enlightened friends of good government are those, whose expectations are the highest.

To justify and preserve their confidence; to promote the encreasing respectability of the American name; to answer the calls of justice; to restore landed property to its due value; to furnish new resources both to agriculture and commerce; to cement more closely the union of the states; to add to their security against foreign attack; to establish public order on the basis of an upright and liberal policy.—These are the great and invaluable ends to be secured, by a proper and adequate provision, at the present period, for the support of public credit.

have to sojourn here, unless called upon
to defend my Country (which every citizen
is bound to do) — but on Public ground also;
for although I have abundant cause to
be thankful for the good health with wh.
I am blessed, yet I am not insensible to my
declination in other respects. — It would
be criminal therefore in me, although
it should be the wish of my Countrymen,
and I could be elected, to accept an Office
under this conviction, which another would
discharge with more ability; — and this too
at a time when I am thoroughly convinced
I should not draw a single vote from the
anti-federal side, and of course, should
stand upon no stronger ground than any
other federal character well supported;
& when I should become a mark for the
shafts of envenomed malice, and the basest calumny to fire at; — when I should
be charged not only with irresolution, but
with concealed ambition, which wants
only an occasion to blaze out; — and, in
short, with dotage and imbecility. —
All this I grant, ought to be like
dust

George Washington to Jonathan Trumbull, July 21, 1799
(The Gilder Lehrman Institute of American History, GLC05787, p. 5)

GEORGE WASHINGTON (1732–1799)

from Letter to Jonathan Trumbull, July 21, 1799

In this letter, written just five months before his death to his former personal secretary, George Washington expresses concern about the potential threat of post-revolutionary France to the United States. Noting the rise of partisanship in American politics, he rejects Federalist pleas that he come out of retirement and run for the presidency in 1800.

No well informed, and unprejudiced man, who has viewed with attention the conduct of the French Government since the Revolution in that Country, can mistake its objects, or the tendency of the ambitious projects it is pursuing. – Yet, strange as it may seem, a party, and a powerful one too, among us, affect to believe that the measures of it are dictated by a principle of self preservation; – that the outrages of which the Directory are guilty, proceed from dire necessity; – that it wishes to be upon the most friendly & amicable terms with the United States; – that it will be the fault of the latter if this is not the case; – that the defensive measures which this Country have adopted, are not only unnecessary & expensive, but have a tendency to produce the evil which, to deprecate, is mere pretence in the Government; because War with France they say, is its wish; – that on the Militia we sh.[d] rest our security; – and that it is time enough to call upon these, when the danger is imminent, & apparent. . . .

I remember well, the conversation which you allude to, – and have not forgot the answer I gave you. – In my judgment it applies with as much force now, as then; nay more, because at that time the line between Parties was not so clearly drawn, and the views of the Opposition, so clearly developed as they are at present . . .

Wherein . . . would lye the difference between the present Gentleman in Office, & Myself? –It would be matter of sore regret to me, if I could believe that a serious tho.[t] was turned towards me as his successor; not only as it respects my ardent wishes to pass through the vale of life in retirem[t], undisturbed in the remnant of the days I have to sojourn here, unless called upon to defend my Country (which every citizen is bound to do) – but on Public ground also; – for although I have abundant cause to be thankful for the good health with wh[h.] I am blessed, – yet I am not insensible to my declination in other respects. – It would be criminal therefore in me, although it should be the wish of my Country men, and I could be elected, to accept an Office under this conviction, which another would discharge with more ability; – and this too at a time when I am thoroughly convinced I should not draw a single vote from the Anti-federal side; and of course, should stand upon no stronger ground then any other Federal character well supported; & when I should become a mark for the shafts of envenomed malice, and the basest calumny to fire at; – when I should be charged not only with irresolution, but with concealed ambition, which wants only an occasion to blaze out; – and, in short, with dotage and imbecility.–

Prudence on my part must arrest any attempt of the well meant, but mistaken views of my friends, to introduce me again into the Chair of Government.

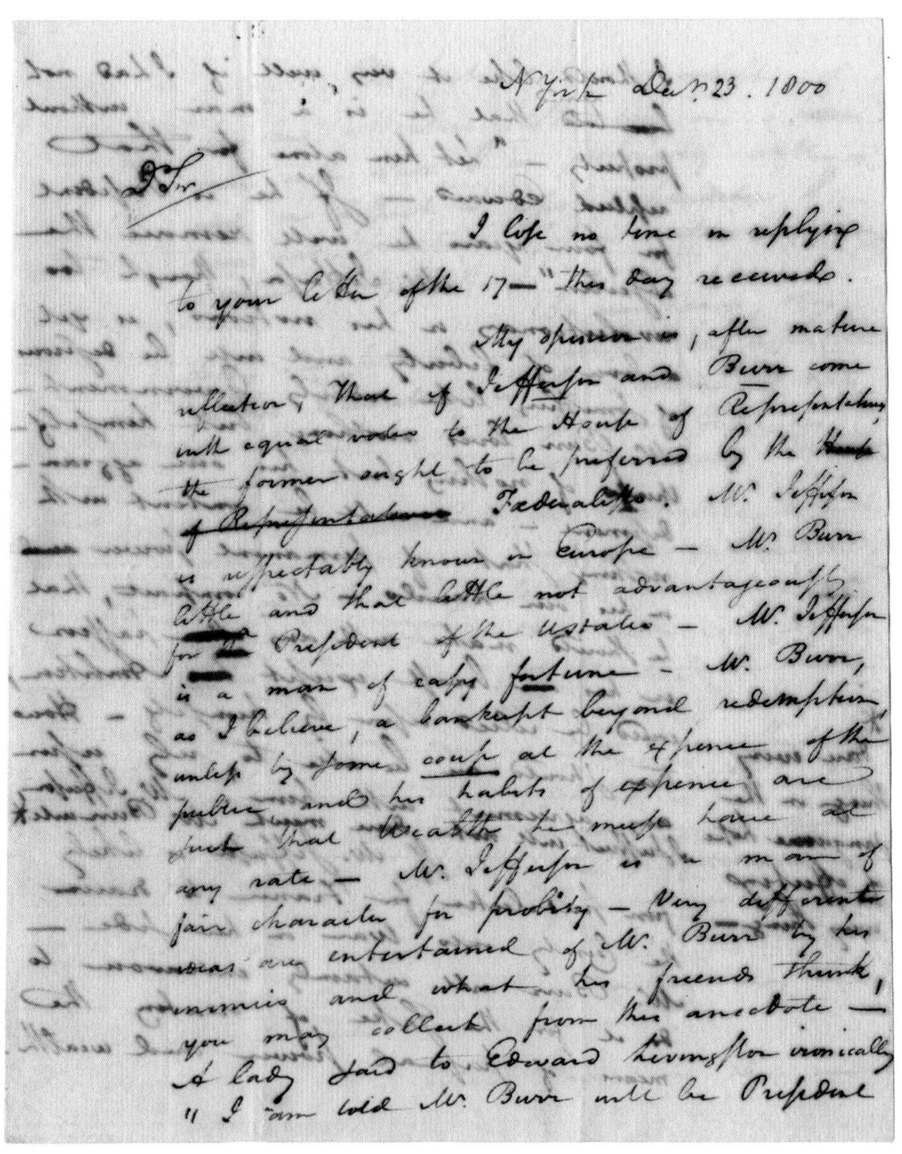

N York Decr 23. 1800

D Sir

I lose no time in replying to your letter of the 17th this day received.

My opinion is, after mature reflection, that if Jefferson and Burr come with equal votes to the House of Representatives the former ought to be preferred by the ~~of Representatives~~ Federalists. Mr. Jefferson is respectably known in Europe — Mr. Burr little and that little not advantageously for President of the U States — Mr. Jefferson is a man of easy fortune — Mr. Burr, as I believe, a bankrupt beyond redemption unless by some coup at the expence of the public and his habits of expence are such that wealth he must have at any rate — Mr. Jefferson is a man of fair character for probity — Very different ideas are entertained of Mr. Burr by his enemies and what his friends think, you may collect from this anecdote — A lady said to Edward Livingston ironically "I am told Mr. Burr will be President

Alexander Hamilton to Harrison Gray Otis, December 23, 1800
(The Gilder Lehrman Institute of American History, GLC00496.028, p. 1)

ALEXANDER HAMILTON (ca. 1757–1804)

from Letter to Harrison Gray Otis, December 23, 1800

The presidential election of 1800 provided Hamilton with a dilemma: a tie between Thomas Jefferson, a man whose principles were in direct opposition to Hamilton's own, and Aaron Burr, a man Hamilton believed to have no principles at all. As the House of Representatives prepared to vote to break the deadlock, Hamilton conducted a furious letter-writing campaign to urge fellow Federalists to vote for Jefferson whom, on balance, Hamilton found "less dangerous than Burr." Burr never forgot that Hamilton had campaigned to deny him the presidency.

N York Decr. 23. 1800

Dr Sir,

I lose no time in replying to your letter of the 17—this day received.

My opinion is, after mature reflection, that if Jefferson and Burr come with equal votes to the House of Representatives, the former ought to be preferred by the Federalists. M^{r}. Jefferson is respectably known in Europe – Mr. Burr little and that little not advantageously for a President of the U States – Mr. Jefferson is a man of easy fortune – Mr. Burr, as I believe, a bankrupt beyond redemption, unless by some coup at the expence of the public, and his habits of expence are such that Wealth he must have at any rate – Mr. Jefferson is a man of fair character for probity. . . . Mr. Jefferson, though too revolutionary in his notions, is yet a lover of liberty and will be desirous of something like orderly Government – Mr. Burr loves nothing but himself – thinks of nothing but his own aggrandizement – and will be content with nothing short of permanent power in his own hands – No compact, that he should make with any passion in his breast except Ambition, could be relied upon by himself – How then should we be able to rely upon any agreement with him? Mr. Jefferson, I suspect will not dare much Mr. Burr will dare every thing in the sanguine hope of effecting every thing –

If Mr. Jefferson is likely from predilection for France to draw the Country into War on her side – Mr. Burr will certainly endeavour to do it for the sake of creating the means of personal power and wealth.

This portrait is the result of long and attentive observation on a man with whom I am personally well – and in respect to whose character I have had peculiar opportunities of forming a correct judgment.

By no means, my Dear Sir, let the Federalists be responsible for his Elevation – In a choice of Evils let them take the least – Jefferson is in every view less dangerous than Burr.

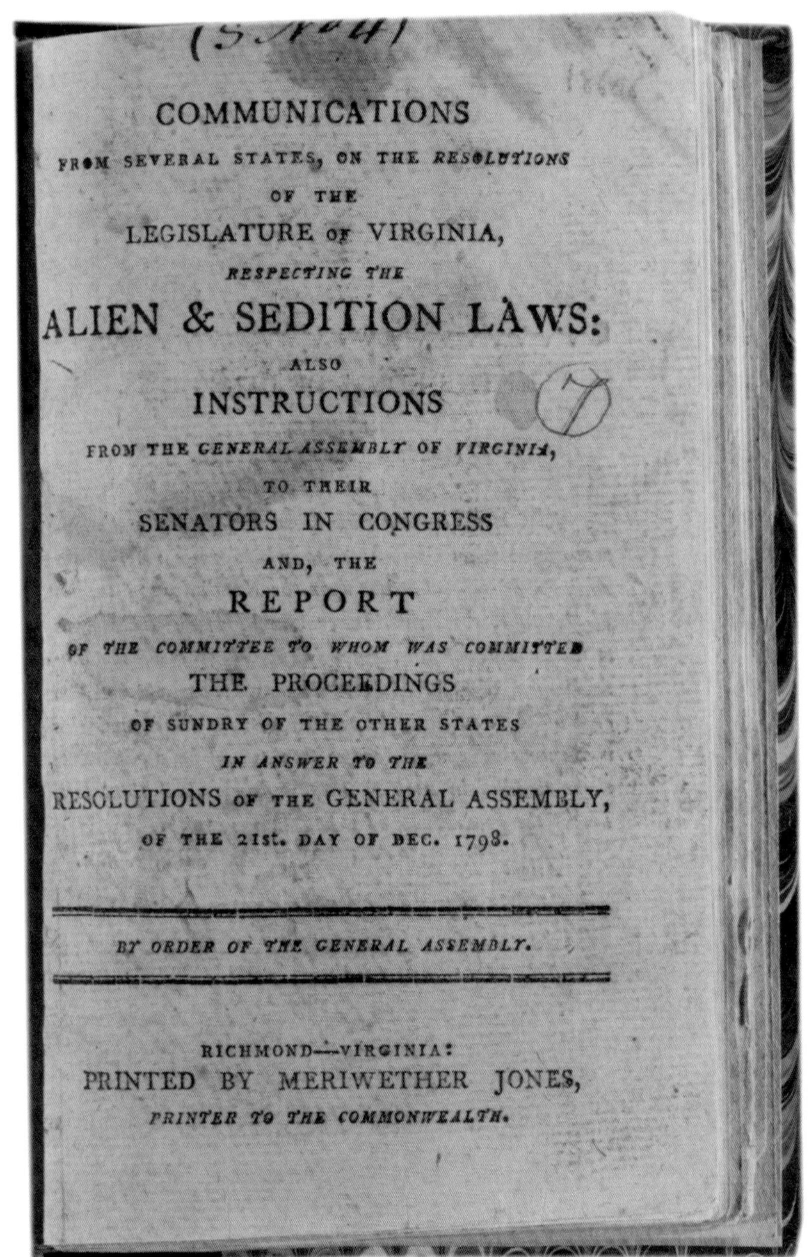

COMMUNICATIONS

FROM SEVERAL STATES, ON THE *RESOLUTIONS*

OF THE

LEGISLATURE OF VIRGINIA,

RESPECTING THE

ALIEN & SEDITION LAWS:

ALSO

INSTRUCTIONS

FROM THE *GENERAL ASSEMBLY* OF *VIRGINIA*,

TO THEIR

SENATORS IN CONGRESS

AND, THE

REPORT

OF THE COMMITTEE TO WHOM WAS COMMITTED

THE PROCEEDINGS

OF SUNDRY OF THE OTHER STATES

IN ANSWER TO THE

RESOLUTIONS OF THE GENERAL ASSEMBLY,

OF THE 21st. DAY OF DEC. 1798.

BY ORDER OF THE GENERAL ASSEMBLY.

RICHMOND—VIRGINIA:

PRINTED BY MERIWETHER JONES,

PRINTER TO THE COMMONWEALTH.

Communications from Several States, on the Resolutions of the Legislature of Virginia, Respecting the Alien & Sedition Laws, 1800
(The Gilder Lehrman Institute of American History, GLC05480)

STATE LEGISLATURES RESPOND TO THE ALIEN AND SEDITION ACTS (1800)

from *Communications from Several States, on the Resolutions of the Legislature of Virginia, Respecting the Alien & Sedition Laws* (Richmond, 1800), pp. 7-9.

The Alien and Sedition Acts, passed by Congress in 1800, were designed to suppress public criticism of the government. These laws lengthened the period necessary before immigrants could become citizens from five to fourteen years, gave the president the power to imprison or deport any foreigner believed to be dangerous to the United States, and made it a crime to attack the government in writing. The state legislatures of Virginia and Kentucky adopted resolutions written by Thomas Jefferson and James Madison denouncing the Alien and Sedition Acts as an infringement on freedom of expression and a usurpation of power.

[T]he United States at the time of passing the *Act concerning Aliens*, were threatened with actual invasion, had been driven by the unjust and ambitious conduct of the French government into warlike preparations expensive and burthensome, and had then within the bosom of the country, thousands of aliens, who, we doubt not, were ready to co-operate in any external attack.

It cannot be seriously believed, that the United States should have waited till the poignard had in fact been plunged. The removal of aliens, is the usual preliminary of hostility, and is justified by the invariable usages of nations. Actual hostility unhappily had long been experienced, and a formal declaration of it, the government had reason daily to expect. The law therefore was just and salutary, and no officer could with so much propriety be entrusted with the execution of it, as the one in whom the Constitution has reposed the executive power of the United States.

The Sedition Act, so called, is, in the opinion of this legislature, equally defensible. The General Assembly of Virginia, in their resolve under consideration, observe, that when that state by its convention ratified the federal constitution, it expressly declared, "That among other essential rights, the liberty of conscience and of the press cannot be cancelled, abridged, restrained or modified by any authority of the United States," and from its extreme anxiety to guard these rights from every possible attack of sophistry or ambition, with other states recommended an amendment for that purpose, which amendment was in due time annexed to the constitution; but they did not surely expect that the proceedings of their state convention were to explain the amendment adopted by the union. The words of that amendment on this subject are, "Congress shall make no law abridging the freedom of speech or of the press."

The act complained of is no abridgement of the freedom of either. The genuine liberty of speech and the press, is the liberty to utter and publish the truth—but the constitutional right of the citizen to utter and publish the truth, is not to be confounded with the licentiousness in speaking and writing, that is only employed in propagating falsehood and slander. This freedom of the press has been expressly secured by most if not all the state constitutions; and of this provision there has been generally but one construction among enlightened men; that it is a security for the rational use and not the abuse of the press; of which the courts of law, the juries and people will judge; this right is not infringed, but confirmed and established by the late act of Congress.

Contributors

Carol Berkin is Presidential Professor of History Emerita at Baruch College and the Graduate Center, City University of New York. She is the author of several books, including *First Generations: Women in Colonial America; A Brilliant Solution: Inventing the American Constitution; Revolutionary Mothers: Women in the Struggle for America's Independence; Civil War Wives: The Lives and Times of Angelina Grimké Weld, Varina Howell Davis, and Julia Dent Grant; Wondrous Beauty: The Life and Adventures of Elizabeth Patterson Bonaparte; The Bill of Rights: The Fight to Secure America's Liberties;* and most recently, *A Sovereign People: The Crises of the 1790s and the Birth of American Nationalism.* Berkin is a frequent contributor to PBS and History Channel television documentaries on early American and Revolutionary era history and edits the Gilder Lehrman Institute's online journal, *History Now.* She serves on the scholarly boards of several professional organizations including the National Women's History Museum and the New-York Historical Society's Center for Women's History.

Denver Brunsman is Associate Professor of History at George Washington University, where his courses include "George Washington and His World," taught annually at Mount Vernon in Virginia. His book *The Evil Necessity: British Naval Impressment in the Eighteenth-Century Atlantic World* received the Walker Cowen Memorial Prize for an outstanding work in eighteenth-century studies in the Americas and Atlantic world. Brunsman is also a co-author of a leading college and AP US History textbook, *Liberty, Equality, Power: A History of the American People*, and an editor of *The American Revolution Reader*, among other works.

Benjamin L. Carp is the Daniel M. Lyons Chair of History and an associate professor of early American history at Brooklyn College of the City University of New York. He is the author of *Defiance of the Patriots: The Boston Tea Party and the Making of America*, which won the Society of the Cincinnati Cox Book Prize in 2013; and *Rebels Rising: Cities and the American Revolution*. Carp is co-editor, with Richard D. Brown, of *Major Problems in the Era of the American Revolution, 1760–1791: Documents and Essays*, third edition. He has written articles on the Revolutionary era for *Early American Studies* and the *William and Mary Quarterly*, among other journals. Carp received the Leverhulme Research Fellowship in 2005 and the Charlotte W Newcombe Doctoral Dissertation Fellowship in 2003.

Julie Silverbrook holds a JD from the William & Mary Law School, where she received the National Association of Women Lawyers Award and the Thurgood Marshall Award and served as a Senior Articles Editor on the *William & Mary Bill of Rights Journal*. Silverbrook was awarded the John C. Morgan Prize by The George Washington University's Department of Political Science, an award given annually to an outstanding graduate pursuing a law degree after graduation. She lectures and presents on the US Constitution and American history at colleges, universities, historical societies, presidential homes, state bar associations, and social studies organizations across the country.

Selected Books for Further Reading

Alexander, Leslie. *African or American?: Black Identity and Political Activism in New York City, 1784–1861.* Urbana-Champaign: University of Illinois Press, 2008.

Allen, Danielle. *Our Declaration: A Reading of the Declaration of Independence in Defense of Equality.* New York: Norton/Liveright, 2014.

Archer, Richard. *As If an Enemy's Country: The British Occupation of Boston and the Origins of Revolution.* New York: Oxford University Press, 2010.

Berkin, Carol. *A Brilliant Solution: Inventing the American Constitution.* Boston: Mariner Books, 2003.

Berkin, Carol. *Revolutionary Mothers: Women in the Struggle for America's Independence.* New York: Vintage Books, 2006.

Bourne, Russell. *Cradle of Violence: How Boston's Waterfront Mobs Ignited the American Revolution.* Hoboken: Wiley, 2006.

Brunsman, Denver, and David J. Silverman, eds. *The American Revolution Reader.* New York: Routledge, 2013.

Brunsman, Denver, and Joel Stone, eds. *Revolutionary Detroit: Portraits in Political and Cultural Change, 1760–1805.* Detroit: Wayne State University Press, 2009.

Calloway, Colin G. *The Indian World of George Washington: The First President, the First Americans, and the Birth of the Nation.* New York: Oxford University Press, 2018.

Carp, Benjamin L. *Rebels Rising: Cities and the American Revolution.* New York: Oxford University Press, 2007.

Carretta, Vincent. *Phillis Wheatley: Biography of a Genius in Bondage.* Athens: University of Georgia Press, 2011.

Ferling, John. *Almost a Miracle: The American Victory in the War of Independence.* New York: Oxford University Press, 2007.

Fischer, David Hackett. *Washington's Crossing.* New York: Oxford University Press, 2004.

Fitz, Caitlin. *Our Sister Republics: The United States in an Age of American Revolutions.* New York: Norton/Liveright, 2016.

Hamilton, Phillip. *The Revolutionary War Lives and Letters of Lucy and Henry Knox.* Baltimore: Johns Hopkins University Press, 2017.

Holton, Woody. *Unruly Americans and the Origins of the Constitution.* New York: Hill and Wang, 2008.

Horne, Gerald. *The Counter-Revolution of 1776: Slave Resistance and the Origins of the United States of America.* New York: New York University Press, 2014.

Jasanoff, Maya. *Liberty's Exiles: American Loyalists in the Revolutionary World.* New York: Vintage Books, 2012.

Kaplan, Sidney, and Emma Nogrady Kaplan, eds. *The Black Presence in the Era of the American Revolution, 1770–1800.* Amherst: University of Massachusetts Press, 1989.

Maier, Pauline. *American Scripture: Making the Declaration of Independence*. New York: Vintage Books, 1998.

Maier, Pauline. *Ratification: The People Debate the Constitution, 1787–1788*. New York: Simon and Schuster, 2010.

McCullough, David. *1776*. New York: Simon and Schuster, 2006.

Philbrick, Nathaniel. *Bunker Hill: A City, a Siege, a Revolution*. New York: Penguin, 2014.

Shorto, Russell. *Revolution Song: A Story of American Freedom*. New York: Norton, 2017.

Slauter, Eric. *The State as a Work of Art: The Cultural Origins of the Constitution*. Chicago: University of Chicago Press, 2009.

Van Buskirk, Judith L. *Standing in Their Own Light: African American Patriots in the American Revolution*. Norman: University of Oklahoma Press, 2017.

Wood, Gordon S. *The American Revolution: A History*. New York: Modern Library, 2003.

Selected Websites for Further Research

The Gilder Lehrman Institute of American History
gilderlehrman.org
A source for original Founding Era documents, essays, digital resources, and more.

Revisiting the Founding Era project site
gilderlehrman.org/programs-and-events/revisiting-founding-era
Features a PDF of *Revisiting the Founding Era: Readings from the Gilder Lehrman Institute of American History*, videos by scholars including Carol Berkin and Denver Brunsman, and an interactive timeline.

Other Online Resources

American Library Association—www.ala.org

EDSITEment—www.edsitement.neh.gov

Library of Congress—www.loc.gov

National Archives—www.archives.gov

National Constitution Center—www.constitutioncenter.org

Smithsonian National Museum of American History—www.americanhistory.si.edu

Appendix

Original Printings of the Declaration of Independence and the US Constitution from the Gilder Lehrman Institute of American History

Today news spreads around the world through television and the internet, but in the eighteenth century, print was the medium for disseminating information and ideas. The Gilder Lehrman Institute's original published copies of the Declaration of Independence and the US Constitution represent the crucial role of the printed word in establishing the foundation of the American republic.

- Declaration of Independence, printed by Peter Timothy, Charleston, South Carolina, August 1776
- Broadsheet printing of the US Constitution, Philadelphia, Pennsylvania, September 17–19, 1787

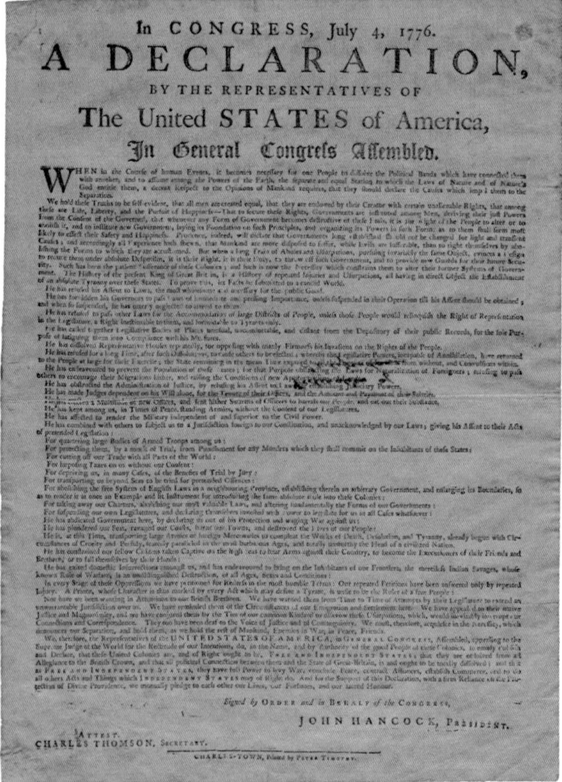

In CONGRESS, July 4, 1776.

A DECLARATION,

BY THE REPRESENTATIVES OF

The United STATES of America,

In General Congress Assembled.

Signed by ORDER and in BEHALF of the CONGRESS,

JOHN HANCOCK, PRESIDENT.

ATTEST.
CHARLES THOMSON, SECRETARY.

CHARLES-TOWN, Printed by PETER TIMOTHY.

Declaration of Independence, printed by Peter Timothy, Charleston, South Carolina, August 1776 (The Gilder Lehrman Institute of American History, GLC00959)

THE DECLARATION OF INDEPENDENCE (1776)

First printed in Philadelphia in July 1776, the Declaration of Independence was then sent to other cities for reprinting and dissemination. This copy, which is the sole survivor of a Charleston, South Carolina, printing in August 1776, did not surface until the 1990s. It is the first concrete proof that such a printing occurred, with the intention of spreading the news of American independence through the South Carolina hinterlands. By publishing his name, the patriotic printer, Peter Timothy, literally put his life on the line.

In CONGRESS, July 4. 1776.
A DECLARATION, BY THE REPRESENTATIVES OF
The United States of America, *In General Congress Assembled.*

WHEN in the Course of human Events, it becomes necessary for one People to dissolve the Political Bands which have connected them with another, and to assume among the Powers of the Earth, the separate and equal Station to which the Laws of Nature and of Nature's God entitle them, a decent Respect to the Opinions of Mankind requires, that they should declare the Causes which impel them to the Separation.

We hold these Truths to be self-evident, that all men are created equal, that they are endowed by their Creator with certain unalienable Rights, that among these are Life, Liberty, and the Pursuit of Happiness—That to secure these Rights, Governments are instituted among Men, deriving their just Powers from the Consent of the Governed, that whenever any Form of Government becomes destructive of these Ends, it is the Right of the People to alter or to abolish it, and to institute new Government, laying its Foundation on such Principles, and organizing its Powers in such Form, as to them shall seem most likely to effect their Safety and Happiness. Prudence, indeed, will dictate that Governments long established should not be changed for light and transient Causes; and accordingly all Experience hath shewn, that Mankind are more disposed to suffer, while Evils are sufferable, than to right themselves by abolishing the Forms to which they are accustomed. But when a long Train of Abuses and Usurpations, pursuing invariably the same Object, evinces a Design to reduce them under absolute Despotism, it is their Right, it is their Duty, to throw off such Government, and to provide new Guards for their future Security. Such has been the patient Sufferance of these Colonies; and such is now the Necessity which constrains them to alter their former Systems of Government. The History of the present King of Great Britain, is a History of repeated Injuries and Usurpations, all having in direct Object the Establishment of an absolute Tyranny over these States. To prove this, let Facts be submitted to a candid World.

He has refused his Assent to Laws, the most wholesome and necessary for the public Good.

He has forbidden his Governors to pass Laws of immediate and pressing Importance, unless suspended in their Operation till his Assent should be obtained, and when so suspended, he has utterly neglected to attend to them.

He has refused to pass other Laws for the Accommodation of large Districts of People, unless those People would relinquish the Right of Representation in the Legislature, a Right inestimable to them, and formidable to Tyrants only.

He has called together Legislative Bodies at Places unusual, uncomfortable, and distant from the Depository of their public Records, for the sole Purpose of fatiguing them into Compliance with his Measures.

He has dissolved Representative Houses repeatedly, for opposing with manly Firmness his Invasions on the Rights of the People.

He has refused for a long Time, after such Dissolutions, to cause others to be elected; whereby the Legislative Powers, incapable of Annihilation, have returned to the People at large for their Exercise; the State remaining in the mean Time exposed to all the Dangers of Invasion from without, and Convulsions within.

He has endeavoured to prevent the Population of these States; for that Purpose obstructing the Laws for Naturalization of Foreigners; refusing to pass others to encourage their Migrations hither, and raising the Conditions of new Appropriations of Lands.

He has obstructed the Administration of Justice, by refusing his Assent to Laws for establishing Judiciary Powers.

He has made Judges dependent on his Will alone, for the Tenure of their Offices, and the Amount and Payment of their Salaries.

He has erected a Multitude of new Offices, and sent hither Swarms of Officers to harass our People, and eat out their Substance.

He has kept among us, in Times of Peace, standing Armies, without the Consent of our Legislatures.

He has affected to render the Military independent of and superior to the Civil Power.

He has combined with others to subject us to a Jurisdiction foreign to our Constitution, and unacknowledged by our Laws; giving his Assent to their Acts of pretended Legislation:

For quartering large Bodies of Armed Troops among us:

For protecting them, by a mock of Trial, from Punishment for any Murders which they shall commit on the Inhabitants of these States:

For cutting off our Trade with all Parts of the World:

For imposing Taxes on us without our Consent:

For depriving us, in many Cases, of the Benefits of Trial by Jury:

For transporting us beyond Seas to be tried for pretend Offences:

For abolishing the free System of English Laws in a neighbouring Province, establishing therein an arbitrary Government, and enlarging its Boundaries, so as to render it at once an Example and fit Instrument for introducing the same absolute Rule into these Colonies:

For taking away our Charters, abolishing our most valuable Laws, and altering fundamentally the Forms of our Governments:

For suspending our own Legislatures, and declaring themselves invested with Power to legislate for us in all Cases whatsoever:

He has abdicated Government here, by declaring us out of his Protection and waging War against us:

He has plundered our Seas, ravaged our Coasts, burnt our Towns, and destroyed the Lives of our People:

He is, at this Time, transporting large Armies of foreign Mercenaries to compleat the Works of Death, Desolation, and Tyranny, already begun with Circumstances of Cruelty and Perfidy, scarcely paralleled in the most barbarous Ages, and totally unworthy the Head of a civilized Nation.

He has constrained our fellow Citizens taken Captive on the High Seas to bear Arms against their Country, to become the Executioners of their Friends and Brethren, or to fall themselves by their Hands:

He has exited domestic Insurrections amongst us, and has endeavoured to bring on the Inhabitants of our Frontiers, the merciless Indian Savages, whose known Rule of Warfare, is an undistinguished Destruction, of all Ages, Sexes and Conditions:

In every Stage of these Oppressions we have petitioned for Redress in the most humble Terms: Our repeated Petitions have been answered only by repeated Injury. A Prince, whose Character is thus marked by every Act which may define a Tyrant, is unfit to be the Ruler of a free People:

Nor have we been wanting in Attentions to our British Brethren. We have warned them from Time to Time of Attempts by their Legislature to extend an unwarrantable Jurisdiction over us. We have reminded them of the Circumstances of our Emigration and Settlement here. We have appealed to their native Justice and Magnanimity, and we have conjured them by the Ties of our common Kindred to disavow these Usurpations, which, would inevitably interrupt our Connections and Correspondence. They too have been deaf to the Voice of Justice and of Consanguinity. We must, therefore, acquiesce in the Necessity, which denounces our Separation, and hold them, as we hold the rest of Mankind, Enemies in War, in Peace, Friends.

We, therefore, the Representatives of the UNITED STATES OF AMERICA, in GENERAL CONGRESS, Assembled, appealing to the Supreme Judge of the World for the Rectitude of our Intentions, do, in the Name, and by Authority of the good People of these Colonies, solemnly Publish and Declare, that these United Colonies are, and of Right ought to be, FREE AND INDEPENDENT STATES; that they are obsolved from all Allegiance to the British Crown, and that all political Connection between them and the State of Great-Britain, is and ought to be totally dissolved; and that as FREE AND INDEPENDENT STATES, they have full Power to levy War, conclude Peace, contract Alliances, establish Commerce, and to do all others Acts and Things which INDEPENDENT STATES may of Right do. And for the Support of this Declaration, with a firm Reliance on the Protection of Divine Providence, we mutually pledge to each other our Lives, our Fortunes, and our sacred Honour.

Signed by ORDER *and in* BEHALF *of the* CONGRESS,
JOHN HANCOCK, PRESIDENT.

ATTEST.
CHARLES THOMSON, SECRETARY.

CHARLES-TOWN, Printed by PETER TIMOTHY

THE US CONSTITUTION (1787)

This is the rarest printing of the US Constitution, with only two copies in existence. It is the first edition printed specifically for mass public circulation.

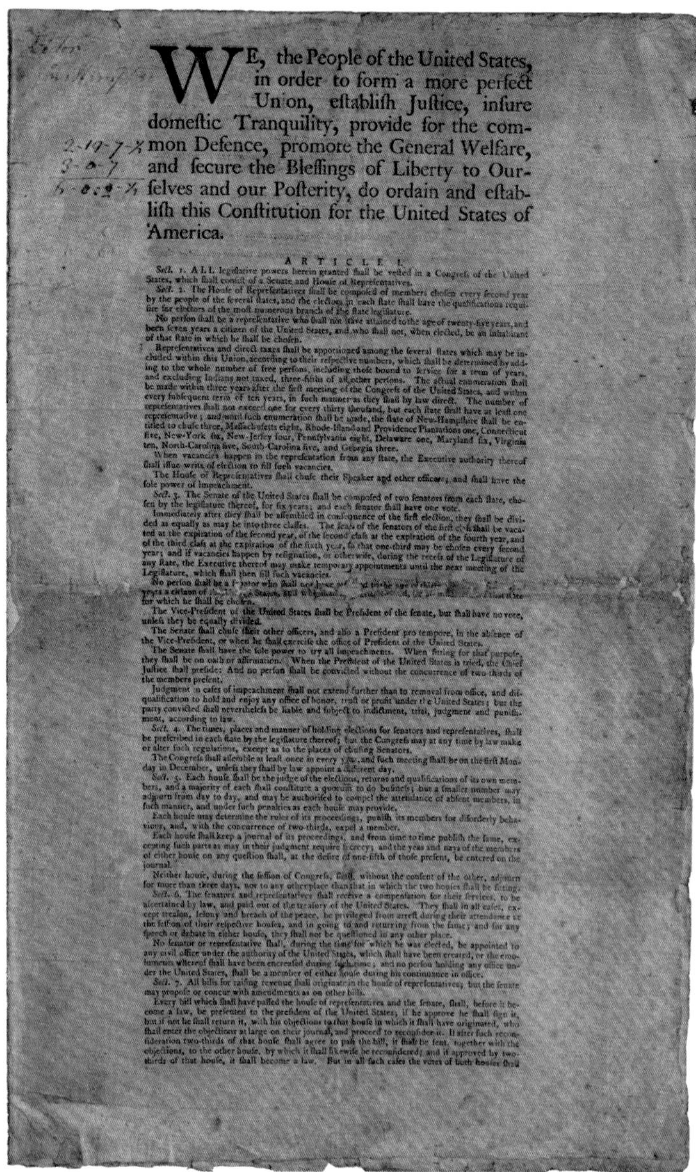

WE, the People of the United States, in order to form a more perfect Union, eſtabliſh Juſtice, inſure domeſtic Tranquility, provide for the common Defence, promote the General Welfare, and ſecure the Bleſſings of Liberty to Ourſelves and our Poſterity, do ordain and eſtabliſh this Conſtitution for the United States of America.

ARTICLE I.

Sect. 1. ALL legiſlative powers herein granted ſhall be veſted in a Congreſs of the United States, which ſhall conſiſt of a Senate and Houſe of Repreſentatives.

Sect. 2. The Houſe of Repreſentatives ſhall be compoſed of members choſen every ſecond year by the people of the ſeveral ſtates, and the electors in each ſtate ſhall have the qualifications requiſite for electors of the moſt numerous branch of the ſtate legiſlature.

No perſon ſhall be a repreſentative who ſhall not have attained to the age of twenty-five years, and been ſeven years a citizen of the United States, and who ſhall not, when elected, be an inhabitant of that ſtate in which he ſhall be choſen.

Repreſentatives and direct taxes ſhall be apportioned among the ſeveral ſtates which may be included within this Union, according to their reſpective numbers, which ſhall be determined by adding to the whole number of free perſons, including thoſe bound to ſervice for a term of years, and excluding Indians not taxed, three-fifths of all other perſons. The actual enumeration ſhall be made within three years after the firſt meeting of the Congreſs of the United States, and within every ſubſequent term of ten years, in ſuch manner as they ſhall by law direct. The number of repreſentatives ſhall not exceed one for every thirty thouſand, but each ſtate ſhall have at leaſt one repreſentative; and until ſuch enumeration ſhall be made, the ſtate of New-Hampſhire ſhall be entitled to chuſe three, Maſſachuſetts eight, Rhode-Iſland and Providence Plantations one, Connecticut five, New-York ſix, New-Jerſey four, Pennſylvania eight, Delaware one, Maryland ſix, Virginia ten, North-Carolina five, South-Carolina five, and Georgia three.

When vacancies happen in the repreſentation from any ſtate, the Executive authority thereof ſhall iſſue writs of election to fill ſuch vacancies.

The Houſe of Repreſentatives ſhall chuſe their Speaker and other officers; and ſhall have the ſole power of impeachment.

Sect. 3. The Senate of the United States ſhall be compoſed of two ſenators from each ſtate, choſen by the legiſlature thereof, for ſix years; and each ſenator ſhall have one vote.

Immediately after they ſhall be aſſembled in conſequence of the firſt election, they ſhall be divided as equally as may be into three claſſes. The ſeats of the ſenators of the firſt claſs ſhall be vacated at the expiration of the ſecond year, of the ſecond claſs at the expiration of the fourth year, and of the third claſs at the expiration of the ſixth year, ſo that one-third may be choſen every ſecond year; and if vacancies happen by reſignation, or otherwiſe, during the receſs of the Legiſlature of any ſtate, the Executive thereof may make temporary appointments until the next meeting of the Legiſlature, which ſhall then fill ſuch vacancies.

No perſon ſhall be a ſenator who ſhall not have [illegible] years a citizen of [illegible] States, and who [illegible] for which he ſhall be choſen.

The Vice-Preſident of the United States ſhall be Preſident of the ſenate, but ſhall have no vote, unleſs they be equally divided.

The Senate ſhall chuſe their other officers, and alſo a Preſident pro tempore, in the abſence of the Vice-Preſident, or when he ſhall exerciſe the office of Preſident of the United States.

The Senate ſhall have the ſole power to try all impeachments. When ſitting for that purpoſe, they ſhall be on oath or affirmation. When the Preſident of the United States is tried, the Chief Juſtice ſhall preſide: And no perſon ſhall be convicted without the concurrence of two thirds of the members preſent.

Judgment in caſes of impeachment ſhall not extend further than to removal from office, and diſqualification to hold and enjoy any office of honor, truſt or profit under the United States; but the party convicted ſhall nevertheleſs be liable and ſubject to indictment, trial, judgment and puniſhment, according to law.

Sect. 4. The times, places and manner of holding elections for ſenators and repreſentatives, ſhall be preſcribed in each ſtate by the legiſlature thereof; but the Congreſs may at any time by law make or alter ſuch regulations, except as to the places of chuſing Senators.

The Congreſs ſhall aſſemble at leaſt once in every year, and ſuch meeting ſhall be on the firſt Monday in December, unleſs they ſhall by law appoint a different day.

Sect. 5. Each houſe ſhall be the judge of the elections, returns and qualifications of its own members, and a majority of each ſhall conſtitute a quorum to do buſineſs; but a ſmaller number may adjourn from day to day, and may be authoriſed to compel the attendance of abſent members, in ſuch manner, and under ſuch penalties as each houſe may provide.

Each houſe may determine the rules of its proceedings, puniſh its members for diſorderly behaviour, and, with the concurrence of two-thirds, expel a member.

Each houſe ſhall keep a journal of its proceedings, and from time to time publiſh the ſame, excepting ſuch parts as may in their judgment require ſecrecy; and the yeas and nays of the members of either houſe on any queſtion ſhall, at the deſire of one-fifth of thoſe preſent, be entered on the journal.

Neither houſe, during the ſeſſion of Congreſs, ſhall, without the conſent of the other, adjourn for more than three days, nor to any other place than that in which the two houſes ſhall be ſitting.

Sect. 6. The ſenators and repreſentatives ſhall receive a compenſation for their ſervices, to be aſcertained by law, and paid out of the treaſury of the United States. They ſhall in all caſes, except treaſon, felony and breach of the peace, be privileged from arreſt during their attendance at the ſeſſion of their reſpective houſes, and in going to and returning from the ſame; and for any ſpeech or debate in either houſe, they ſhall not be queſtioned in any other place.

No ſenator or repreſentative ſhall, during the time for which he was elected, be appointed to any civil office under the authority of the United States, which ſhall have been created, or the emoluments whereof ſhall have been encreaſed during ſuch time; and no perſon holding any office under the United States, ſhall be a member of either houſe during his continuance in office.

Sect. 7. All bills for raiſing revenue ſhall originate in the houſe of repreſentatives; but the ſenate may propoſe or concur with amendments as on other bills.

Every bill which ſhall have paſſed the houſe of repreſentatives and the ſenate, ſhall, before it become a law, be preſented to the preſident of the United States; if he approve he ſhall ſign it, but if not he ſhall return it, with his objections to that houſe in which it ſhall have originated, who ſhall enter the objections at large on their journal, and proceed to reconſider it. If after ſuch reconſideration two-thirds of that houſe ſhall agree to paſs the bill, it ſhall be ſent, together with the objections, to the other houſe, by which it ſhall likewiſe be reconſidered; and if approved by two-thirds of that houſe, it ſhall become a law. But in all ſuch caſes the votes of both houſes ſhall

Broadsheet printing of the US Constitution, Philadelphia, Pennsylvania, September 17–19, 1787 (The Gilder Lehrman Institute of American History, GLC00258, p. 1)

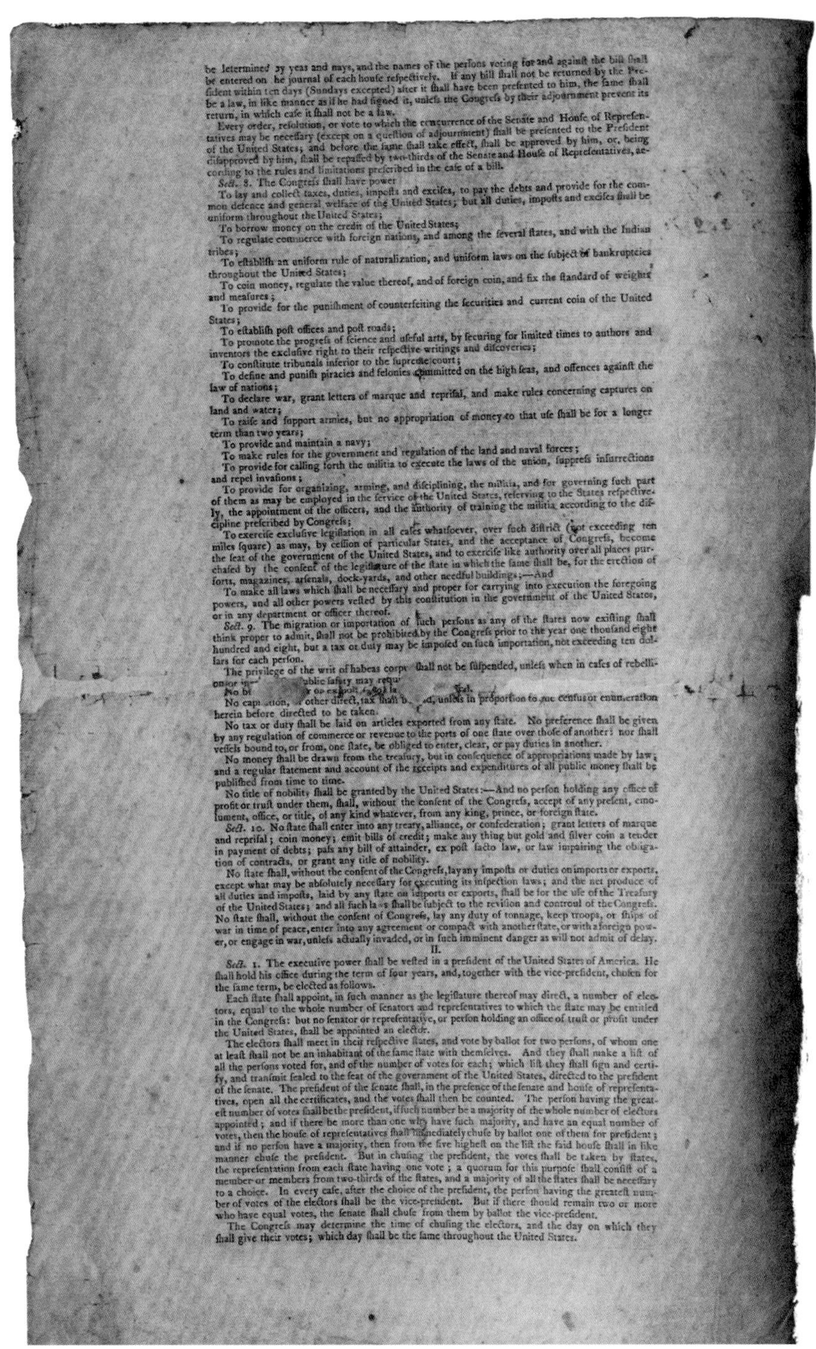

be determined by yeas and nays, and the names of the persons voting for and against the bill shall be entered on the journal of each house respectively. If any bill shall not be returned by the President within ten days (Sundays excepted) after it shall have been presented to him, the same shall be a law, in like manner as if he had signed it, unless the Congress by their adjournment prevent its return, in which case it shall not be a law.

Every order, resolution, or vote to which the concurrence of the Senate and House of Representatives may be necessary (except on a question of adjournment) shall be presented to the President of the United States; and before the same shall take effect, shall be approved by him, or, being disapproved by him, shall be repassed by two-thirds of the Senate and House of Representatives, according to the rules and limitations prescribed in the case of a bill.

Sect. 8. The Congress shall have power

To lay and collect taxes, duties, imposts and excises, to pay the debts and provide for the common defence and general welfare of the United States; but all duties, imposts and excises shall be uniform throughout the United States;

To borrow money on the credit of the United States;

To regulate commerce with foreign nations, and among the several states, and with the Indian tribes;

To establish an uniform rule of naturalization, and uniform laws on the subject of bankruptcies throughout the United States;

To coin money, regulate the value thereof, and of foreign coin, and fix the standard of weights and measures;

To provide for the punishment of counterfeiting the securities and current coin of the United States;

To establish post offices and post roads;

To promote the progress of science and useful arts, by securing for limited times to authors and inventors the exclusive right to their respective writings and discoveries;

To constitute tribunals inferior to the supreme court;

To define and punish piracies and felonies committed on the high seas, and offences against the law of nations;

To declare war, grant letters of marque and reprisal, and make rules concerning captures on land and water;

To raise and support armies, but no appropriation of money to that use shall be for a longer term than two years;

To provide and maintain a navy;

To make rules for the government and regulation of the land and naval forces;

To provide for calling forth the militia to execute the laws of the union, suppress insurrections and repel invasions;

To provide for organizing, arming, and disciplining, the militia, and for governing such part of them as may be employed in the service of the United States, reserving to the States respectively, the appointment of the officers, and the authority of training the militia according to the discipline prescribed by Congress;

To exercise exclusive legislation in all cases whatsoever, over such district (not exceeding ten miles square) as may, by cession of particular States, and the acceptance of Congress, become the seat of the government of the United States, and to exercise like authority over all places purchased by the consent of the legislature of the state in which the same shall be, for the erection of forts, magazines, arsenals, dock-yards, and other needful buildings;—And

To make all laws which shall be necessary and proper for carrying into execution the foregoing powers, and all other powers vested by this constitution in the government of the United States, or in any department or officer thereof.

Sect. 9. The migration or importation of such persons as any of the states now existing shall think proper to admit, shall not be prohibited by the Congress prior to the year one thousand eight hundred and eight, but a tax or duty may be imposed on such importation, not exceeding ten dollars for each person.

The privilege of the writ of habeas corp[illegible] shall not be suspended, unless when in cases of rebellion or in[illegible]ublic safety may requ[illegible]

No b[illegible]r ex post [illegible] la[illegible]sed.

No cap[illegible]ation, [illegible] other direct, tax shall b[illegible]d, unless in proportion to the census or enumeration herein before directed to be taken.

No tax or duty shall be laid on articles exported from any state. No preference shall be given by any regulation of commerce or revenue to the ports of one state over those of another: nor shall vessels bound to, or from, one state, be obliged to enter, clear, or pay duties in another.

No money shall be drawn from the treasury, but in consequence of appropriations made by law; and a regular statement and account of the receipts and expenditures of all public money shall be published from time to time.

No title of nobility shall be granted by the United States:—And no person holding any office of profit or trust under them, shall, without the consent of the Congress, accept of any present, emolument, office, or title, of any kind whatever, from any king, prince, or foreign state.

Sect. 10. No state shall enter into any treaty, alliance, or confederation; grant letters of marque and reprisal; coin money; emit bills of credit; make any thing but gold and silver coin a tender in payment of debts; pass any bill of attainder, ex post facto law, or law impairing the obligation of contracts, or grant any title of nobility.

No state shall, without the consent of the Congress, lay any imposts or duties on imports or exports, except what may be absolutely necessary for executing its inspection laws; and the net produce of all duties and imposts, laid by any state on imports or exports, shall be for the use of the Treasury of the United States; and all such laws shall be subject to the revision and controul of the Congress. No state shall, without the consent of Congress, lay any duty of tonnage, keep troops, or ships of war in time of peace, enter into any agreement or compact with another state, or with a foreign power, or engage in war, unless actually invaded, or in such imminent danger as will not admit of delay.

II.

Sect. 1. The executive power shall be vested in a president of the United States of America. He shall hold his office during the term of four years, and, together with the vice-president, chosen for the same term, be elected as follows.

Each state shall appoint, in such manner as the legislature thereof may direct, a number of electors, equal to the whole number of senators and representatives to which the state may be entitled in the Congress: but no senator or representative, or person holding an office of trust or profit under the United States, shall be appointed an elector.

The electors shall meet in their respective states, and vote by ballot for two persons, of whom one at least shall not be an inhabitant of the same state with themselves. And they shall make a list of all the persons voted for, and of the number of votes for each; which list they shall sign and certify, and transmit sealed to the seat of the government of the United States, directed to the president of the senate. The president of the senate shall, in the presence of the senate and house of representatives, open all the certificates, and the votes shall then be counted. The person having the greatest number of votes shall be the president, if such number be a majority of the whole number of electors appointed; and if there be more than one who have such majority, and have an equal number of votes, then the house of representatives shall immediately chuse by ballot one of them for president; and if no person have a majority, then from the five highest on the list the said house shall in like manner chuse the president. But in chusing the president, the votes shall be taken by states, the representation from each state having one vote; a quorum for this purpose shall consist of a member or members from two-thirds of the states, and a majority of all the states shall be necessary to a choice. In every case, after the choice of the president, the person having the greatest number of votes of the electors shall be the vice-president. But if there should remain two or more who have equal votes, the senate shall chuse from them by ballot the vice-president.

The Congress may determine the time of chusing the electors, and the day on which they shall give their votes; which day shall be the same throughout the United States.

Broadsheet printing of the US Constitution, September 17–19, 1787 (GLC00258, p. 2)

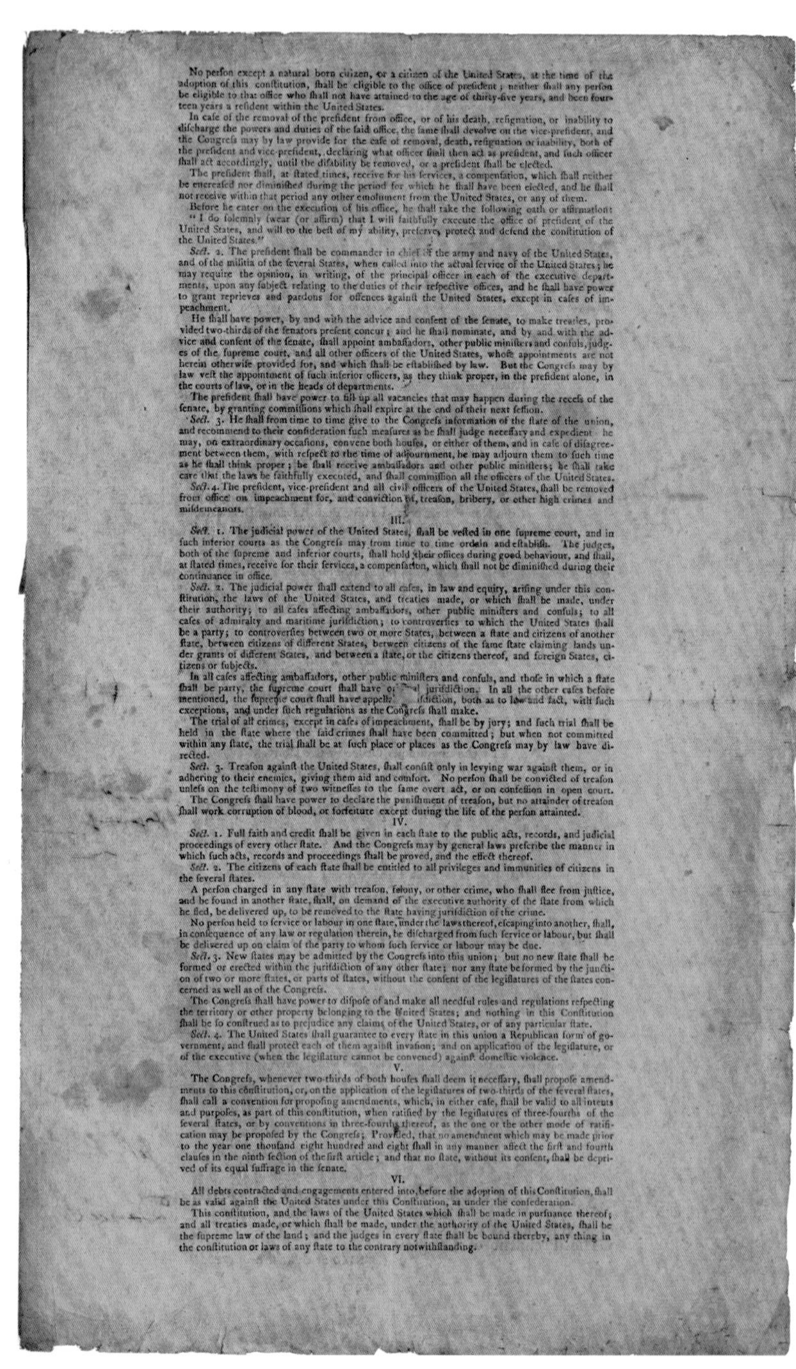

No perſon except a natural born citizen, or a citizen of the United States, at the time of the adoption of this conſtitution, ſhall be eligible to the office of preſident; neither ſhall any perſon be eligible to that office who ſhall not have attained to the age of thirty-five years, and been fourteen years a reſident within the United States.

In caſe of the removal of the preſident from office, or of his death, reſignation, or inability to diſcharge the powers and duties of the ſaid office, the ſame ſhall devolve on the vice-preſident, and the Congreſs may by law provide for the caſe of removal, death, reſignation or inability, both of the preſident and vice-preſident, declaring what officer ſhall then act as preſident, and ſuch officer ſhall act accordingly, until the diſability be removed, or a preſident ſhall be elected.

The preſident ſhall, at ſtated times, receive for his ſervices, a compenſation, which ſhall neither be encreaſed nor diminiſhed during the period for which he ſhall have been elected, and he ſhall not receive within that period any other emolument from the United States, or any of them.

Before he enter on the execution of his office, he ſhall take the following oath or affirmation: "I do ſolemnly ſwear (or affirm) that I will faithfully execute the office of preſident of the United States, and will to the beſt of my ability, preſerve, protect and defend the conſtitution of the United States."

Sect. 2. The preſident ſhall be commander in chief of the army and navy of the United States, and of the militia of the ſeveral States, when called into the actual ſervice of the United States; he may require the opinion, in writing, of the principal officer in each of the executive departments, upon any ſubject relating to the duties of their reſpective offices, and he ſhall have power to grant reprieves and pardons for offences againſt the United States, except in caſes of impeachment.

He ſhall have power, by and with the advice and conſent of the ſenate, to make treaties, provided two-thirds of the ſenators preſent concur; and he ſhall nominate, and by and with the advice and conſent of the ſenate, ſhall appoint ambaſſadors, other public miniſters and conſuls, judges of the ſupreme court, and all other officers of the United States, whoſe appointments are not herein otherwiſe provided for, and which ſhall be eſtabliſhed by law. But the Congreſs may by law veſt the appointment of ſuch inferior officers, as they think proper, in the preſident alone, in the courts of law, or in the heads of departments.

The preſident ſhall have power to fill up all vacancies that may happen during the receſs of the ſenate, by granting commiſſions which ſhall expire at the end of their next ſeſſion.

Sect. 3. He ſhall from time to time give to the Congreſs information of the ſtate of the union, and recommend to their conſideration ſuch meaſures as he ſhall judge neceſſary and expedient he may, on extraordinary occaſions, convene both houſes, or either of them, and in caſe of diſagreement between them, with reſpect to the time of adjournment, he may adjourn them to ſuch time as he ſhall think proper; he ſhall receive ambaſſadors and other public miniſters; he ſhall take care that the laws be faithfully executed, and ſhall commiſſion all the officers of the United States.

Sect. 4. The preſident, vice-preſident and all civil officers of the United States, ſhall be removed from office on impeachment for, and conviction of, treaſon, bribery, or other high crimes and miſdemeanors.

III.

Sect. 1. The judicial power of the United States, ſhall be veſted in one ſupreme court, and in ſuch inferior courts as the Congreſs may from time to time ordain and eſtabliſh. The judges, both of the ſupreme and inferior courts, ſhall hold their offices during good behaviour, and ſhall, at ſtated times, receive for their ſervices, a compenſation, which ſhall not be diminiſhed during their continuance in office.

Sect. 2. The judicial power ſhall extend to all caſes, in law and equity, ariſing under this conſtitution, the laws of the United States, and treaties made, or which ſhall be made, under their authority; to all caſes affecting ambaſſadors, other public miniſters and conſuls; to all caſes of admiralty and maritime juriſdiction; to controverſies to which the United States ſhall be a party; to controverſies between two or more States, between a ſtate and citizens of another ſtate, between citizens of different States, between citizens of the ſame ſtate claiming lands under grants of different States, and between a ſtate, or the citizens thereof, and foreign States, citizens or ſubjects.

In all caſes affecting ambaſſadors, other public miniſters and conſuls, and thoſe in which a ſtate ſhall be party, the ſupreme court ſhall have o[illegible]l juriſdiction. In all the other caſes before mentioned, the ſupreme court ſhall have appell[illegible]diction, both as to law and fact, with ſuch exceptions, and under ſuch regulations as the Congreſs ſhall make.

The trial of all crimes, except in caſes of impeachment, ſhall be by jury; and ſuch trial ſhall be held in the ſtate where the ſaid crimes ſhall have been committed; but when not committed within any ſtate, the trial ſhall be at ſuch place or places as the Congreſs may by law have directed.

Sect. 3. Treaſon againſt the United States, ſhall conſiſt only in levying war againſt them, or in adhering to their enemies, giving them aid and comfort. No perſon ſhall be convicted of treaſon unleſs on the teſtimony of two witneſſes to the ſame overt act, or on confeſſion in open court.

The Congreſs ſhall have power to declare the puniſhment of treaſon, but no attainder of treaſon ſhall work corruption of blood, or forfeiture except during the life of the perſon attainted.

IV.

Sect. 1. Full faith and credit ſhall be given in each ſtate to the public acts, records, and judicial proceedings of every other ſtate. And the Congreſs may by general laws preſcribe the manner in which ſuch acts, records and proceedings ſhall be proved, and the effect thereof.

Sect. 2. The citizens of each ſtate ſhall be entitled to all privileges and immunities of citizens in the ſeveral ſtates.

A perſon charged in any ſtate with treaſon, felony, or other crime, who ſhall flee from juſtice, and be found in another ſtate, ſhall, on demand of the executive authority of the ſtate from which he fled, be delivered up, to be removed to the ſtate having juriſdiction of the crime.

No perſon held to ſervice or labour in one ſtate, under the laws thereof, eſcaping into another, ſhall, in conſequence of any law or regulation therein, be diſcharged from ſuch ſervice or labour, but ſhall be delivered up on claim of the party to whom ſuch ſervice or labour may be due.

Sect. 3. New ſtates may be admitted by the Congreſs into this union; but no new ſtate ſhall be formed or erected within the juriſdiction of any other ſtate; nor any ſtate be formed by the junction of two or more ſtates, or parts of ſtates, without the conſent of the legiſlatures of the ſtates concerned as well as of the Congreſs.

The Congreſs ſhall have power to diſpoſe of and make all needful rules and regulations reſpecting the territory or other property belonging to the United States; and nothing in this Conſtitution ſhall be ſo conſtrued as to prejudice any claims of the United States, or of any particular ſtate.

Sect. 4. The United States ſhall guarantee to every ſtate in this union a Republican form of government, and ſhall protect each of them againſt invaſion; and on application of the legiſlature, or of the executive (when the legiſlature cannot be convened) againſt domeſtic violence.

V.

The Congreſs, whenever two-thirds of both houſes ſhall deem it neceſſary, ſhall propoſe amendments to this conſtitution, or, on the application of the legiſlatures of two-thirds of the ſeveral ſtates, ſhall call a convention for propoſing amendments, which, in either caſe, ſhall be valid to all intents and purpoſes, as part of this conſtitution, when ratified by the legiſlatures of three-fourths of the ſeveral ſtates, or by conventions in three-fourths thereof, as the one or the other mode of ratification may be propoſed by the Congreſs; Provided, that no amendment which may be made prior to the year one thouſand eight hundred and eight ſhall in any manner affect the firſt and fourth clauſes in the ninth ſection of the firſt article; and that no ſtate, without its conſent, ſhall be deprived of its equal ſuffrage in the ſenate.

VI.

All debts contracted and engagements entered into, before the adoption of this Conſtitution, ſhall be as valid againſt the United States under this Conſtitution, as under the confederation.

This conſtitution, and the laws of the United States which ſhall be made in purſuance thereof; and all treaties made, or which ſhall be made, under the authority of the United States, ſhall be the ſupreme law of the land; and the judges in every ſtate ſhall be bound thereby, any thing in the conſtitution or laws of any ſtate to the contrary notwithſtanding.

Broadsheet printing of the US Constitution, September 17–19, 1787 (GLC00258, p. 3)

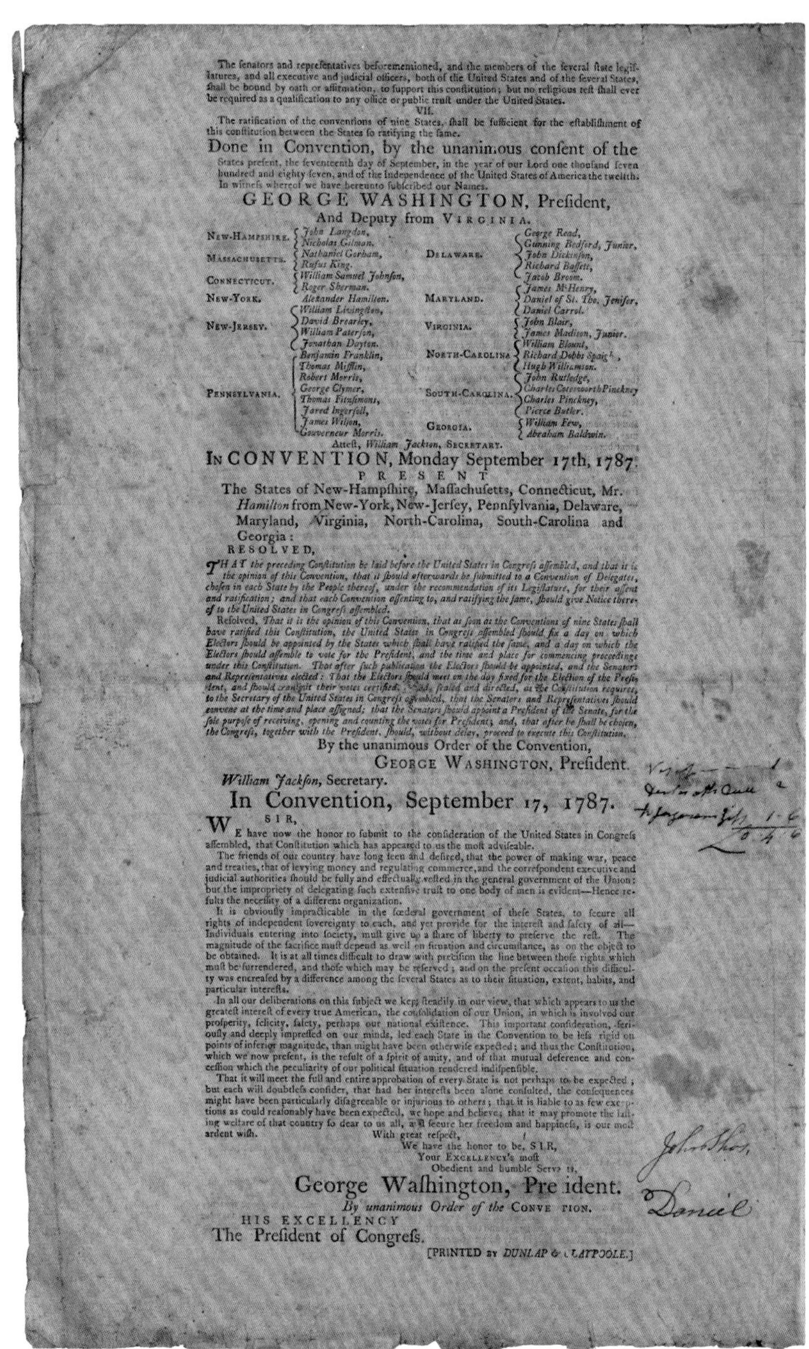

The ſenators and repreſentatives beforementioned, and the members of the ſeveral ſtate legiſlatures, and all executive and judicial officers, both of the United States and of the ſeveral States, ſhall be bound by oath or affirmation, to ſupport this conſtitution; but no religious teſt ſhall ever be required as a qualification to any office or public truſt under the United States.

VII.

The ratification of the conventions of nine States, ſhall be ſufficient for the eſtabliſhment of this conſtitution between the States ſo ratifying the ſame.

Done in Convention, by the unanimous conſent of the States preſent, the ſeventeenth day of September, in the year of our Lord one thouſand ſeven hundred and eighty-ſeven, and of the Independence of the United States of America the twelfth. In witneſs whereof we have hereunto ſubſcribed our Names.

GEORGE WASHINGTON, Preſident,
And Deputy from VIRGINIA.

NEW-HAMPSHIRE.	*John Langdon,* *Nicholas Gilman.*	DELAWARE.	*George Read,* *Gunning Bedford, Junior,* *John Dickinſon,* *Richard Baſſett,* *Jacob Broom.*
MASSACHUSETTS.	*Nathaniel Gorham,* *Rufus King.*	MARYLAND.	*James M'Henry,* *Daniel of St. Tho. Jeniſer,* *Daniel Carrol.*
CONNECTICUT.	*William Samuel Johnſon,* *Roger Sherman.*	VIRGINIA.	*John Blair,* *James Madiſon, Junior.*
NEW-YORK.	*Alexander Hamilton.*	NORTH-CAROLINA.	*William Blount,* *Richard Dobbs Spaight,* *Hugh Williamſon.*
NEW-JERSEY.	*William Livingſton,* *David Brearley,* *William Paterſon,* *Jonathan Dayton.*	SOUTH-CAROLINA.	*John Rutledge,* *Charles Coteſworth Pinckney,* *Charles Pinckney,* *Pierce Butler.*
PENNSYLVANIA.	*Benjamin Franklin,* *Thomas Mifflin,* *Robert Morris,* *George Clymer,* *Thomas Fitzſimons,* *Jared Ingerſoll,* *James Wilſon,* *Gouverneur Morris.*	GEORGIA.	*William Few,* *Abraham Baldwin.*

Atteſt, *William Jackſon*, SECRETARY.

IN CONVENTION, Monday September 17th, 1787.

PRESENT

The States of New-Hampſhire, Maſſachuſetts, Connecticut, Mr. *Hamilton* from New-York, New-Jerſey, Pennſylvania, Delaware, Maryland, Virginia, North-Carolina, South-Carolina and Georgia:

RESOLVED,

THAT the preceding Conſtitution be laid before the United States in Congreſs aſſembled, and that it is the opinion of this Convention, that it ſhould afterwards be ſubmitted to a Convention of Delegates, choſen in each State by the People thereof, under the recommendation of its Legiſlature, for their aſſent and ratification; and that each Convention aſſenting to, and ratifying the ſame, ſhould give Notice thereof to the United States in Congreſs aſſembled.

Reſolved, *That it is the opinion of this Convention, that as ſoon as the Conventions of nine States ſhall have ratified this Conſtitution, the United States in Congreſs aſſembled ſhould fix a day on which Electors ſhould be appointed by the States which ſhall have ratified the ſame, and a day on which the Electors ſhould aſſemble to vote for the Preſident, and the time and place for commencing proceedings under this Conſtitution. That after ſuch publication the Electors ſhould be appointed, and the Senators and Repreſentatives elected: That the Electors ſhould meet on the day fixed for the Election of the Preſident, and ſhould tranſmit their votes certified, ſigned, ſealed and directed, as the Conſtitution requires, to the Secretary of the United States in Congreſs aſſembled, that the Senators and Repreſentatives ſhould convene at the time and place aſſigned; that the Senators ſhould appoint a Preſident of the Senate, for the ſole purpoſe of receiving, opening and counting the votes for Preſident; and, that after he ſhall be choſen, the Congreſs, together with the Preſident, ſhould, without delay, proceed to execute this Conſtitution.*

By the unanimous Order of the Convention,

GEORGE WASHINGTON, Preſident.

William Jackſon, Secretary.

In Convention, September 17, 1787.

SIR,

WE have now the honor to ſubmit to the conſideration of the United States in Congreſs aſſembled, that Conſtitution which has appeared to us the moſt adviſeable.

The friends of our country have long ſeen and deſired, that the power of making war, peace and treaties, that of levying money and regulating commerce, and the correſpondent executive and judicial authorities ſhould be fully and effectually veſted in the general government of the Union: but the impropriety of delegating ſuch extenſive truſt to one body of men is evident—Hence reſults the neceſſity of a different organization.

It is obviouſly impracticable in the fœderal government of theſe States, to ſecure all rights of independent ſovereignty to each, and yet provide for the intereſt and ſafety of all—Individuals entering into ſociety, muſt give up a ſhare of liberty to preſerve the reſt. The magnitude of the ſacrifice muſt depend as well on ſituation and circumſtance, as on the object to be obtained. It is at all times difficult to draw with preciſion the line between thoſe rights which muſt be ſurrendered, and thoſe which may be reſerved; and on the preſent occaſion this difficulty was encreaſed by a difference among the ſeveral States as to their ſituation, extent, habits, and particular intereſts.

In all our deliberations on this ſubject we kept ſteadily in our view, that which appears to us the greateſt intereſt of every true American, the conſolidation of our Union, in which is involved our proſperity, felicity, ſafety, perhaps our national exiſtence. This important conſideration, ſeriouſly and deeply impreſſed on our minds, led each State in the Convention to be leſs rigid on points of inferior magnitude, than might have been otherwiſe expected; and thus the Conſtitution, which we now preſent, is the reſult of a ſpirit of amity, and of that mutual deference and conceſſion which the peculiarity of our political ſituation rendered indiſpenſible.

That it will meet the full and entire approbation of every State is not perhaps to be expected; but each will doubtleſs conſider, that had her intereſts been alone conſulted, the conſequences might have been particularly diſagreeable or injurious to others; that it is liable to as few exceptions as could reaſonably have been expected, we hope and believe; that it may promote the laſting welfare of that country ſo dear to us all, and ſecure her freedom and happineſs, is our moſt ardent wiſh.

With great reſpect,
We have the honor to be, SIR,
Your EXCELLENCY's moſt
Obedient and humble Servants,

George Waſhington, Preſident.
By unanimous Order of the CONVENTION.

HIS EXCELLENCY
The Preſident of Congreſs.

[PRINTED BY *DUNLAP & CLAYPOOLE.*]

Broadsheet printing of the US Constitution, September 17–19, 1787 (GLC00258, p. 4)